W9-BCQ-307

The U.S. Rapid Deployment Forces

The U.S. Rapid Deployment Forces

David Eshel

ARCO Publishing, Inc.
New York

Contents

Editor: Lt. Col. David Eshel (IDF ret.)
Editorial Contributor and Research: Tamir Eshel

Editorial coordinator: Lawrence D. Rifkin
Graphic Design: Jaap Tuinstra

Published by Arco Publishing Inc., 215 Park Avenue South, New York, NY 10003

Copyright © 1985 by Lt. Col. David Eshel

All rights reserved. No part of this book may be reproduced, by any means, without permission in writing from the publisher, except by a reviewer, who wishes to quote brief excerpts in connection with a review in a magazine or newspaper.

Library of Congress Cataloging in Publication Data

Eshel, David.
The U.S. Rapid Deployment Forces.

1. United States. Rapid Deployment Force.
I. Title.
UA23.E76   1984   355.3'5   84-6438

ISBN 0-668-06278-9 paperback

Color: Reshet Kav, Migvan

Printed in the Netherlands by Van Boekhoven-Bosch b.v., Utrecht

The Gulf on Fire

Introduction to the scenario

The opening scenario was not intended as a fortune-telling essay. It was prepared to enable the reader to properly understand the importance of each part of the rapid deployment force. As the reader makes his way through the scenario, he will appreciate the minute problems of rapid deployment and the importance of early warning and fast decision making based on real time intelligence.

A great deal of research went into the scenario, and writing it turned out to be the hardest part of the preparation of this book. The 'action' spans only four days, despite the fact that even the most optimistic reports do not see US rapid deployment units arriving in the Middle East in under 48 hours. We tried to 'squeeze' things, mainly for the sake of a flowing story. If the scenario were for real, everyone involved would most likely face an even worse situation.

I would like to thank Yosef Kostiner, of the Shiloah Institute in Tel Aviv for his help with the scenario's political and ethnographic background, and Lawrence Rifkin and Tamir Eshel for writing it.   D.E.

Scenario

The US troops leave Lebanon, a critical view of US reliability in the Mid East as taken from the Arab Press...

Since 1981, Shi'ite Moslem underground movements in the Gulf region were active in attemps to bring Islamic fundamentalism to fever pitch. They were inspired by the Iranian revolution and, later, by extremist PLO factions which rebelled against Yasser Arafat in Lebanon.

As a by-product of this upheaval, the fundamentalists thought that the US would have to get involved, with the most likely consequences being more of what happened to American troops in Lebanon during 1983, and possibly a decision by Washington to sit down with, and even recognize, the PLO.

The seeds planted by the fundamentalists began to bear fruit in January. Kuwait's 200,000 Shi'ites, some 30 per cent of the country's population, and many of the local Palestinians began moving against what was seen to be an anti-Islamic regime. On the island of Bahrain, about 400 miles to the south, the country's almost 130,000 Shi'ites, about 60 per cent of the population, followed the lead of the Kuwaitis.

The effort in Bahrain was a success, and the strike, fully supported by the island's Shi'ite-controlled unions, was total. In Kuwait, the anti-government moves were widespread, but not total; the army retained at least partial control of the country and a showdown appeared inevitable.

One thousand miles to the south of Kuwait, the defense minister of the People's Democratic Republic of Yemen helped topple his country's three-man ruling triumvirate which had ended hostilities with North Yemen and Oman, traditional enemies of South Yemen. The new rulers contacted Libya, allies in the revolution, and invited its armed forces to take part in military maneuvers in February at the edge of the great Rub al-Khali desert on the PDRY-Saudi Arabian border. The South Yemenis had signed a three-way defense pact with Libya and Ethiopia in 1981, and joint maneuvers would not appear out of the ordinary. The Libyans agreed and sent a mechanized battalion supported by tanks, artillery, helicopters, and a composite squadron of SU-22 and MiG-27 attack aircraft. The maneuvers, totalling three battalions, were dubbed Exercise Friendship. The new PDRY strongmen assured their neighbors that South Yemen had no intention of holding anything but maneuvers, and three weeks later intelligence reports confirmed that the exercise was over, and the forces had withdrawn from the area.

Note: All hours listed in parenthesis next to the locations are LOCAL TIME.

AL KUWAIT

All hell breaks loose. Tens of thousands of Shi'ites and Moslem fundamentalists take to the streets, burning tires, smashing the windows of liquor stores and screaming 'Death to Western imperialism.' The international airport is overrun and nearby radar facilities are destroyed. Television and radio stations are taken over, and fundamentalist leaders broadcast revolutionary exhortations and call for assistance from their brothers in Iran. Security forces clash with the crowds. Shots ring out and people on both sides of the barricades fall to the ground. Parliament is besieged as it sits in emergency session; the decision is taken to call for help from the Gulf Cooperation Council, and contact is made just before Kuwait's main telephone lines to the outside world are cut.

BUSHIR AIR BASE, IRAN

The upheaval in Kuwait did not begin by chance; fundamentalists in Iran even knew the hour it would start, and thus hundreds of Mujahedin have been waiting here for a call to help their brethren across the Gulf. The radio broadcasts from the Kuwaiti rebels blare from loudspeakers around the base: 'This is the radio of the Islamic Republic of Kuwait.' The order comes from Teheran, and the revolutionary guards board their Hercules aircraft.

BAHRAIN

Immediately upon hearing Kuwaiti rebel broadcasts, Bahrainian Shi'ites take to the strike-bound island's empty streets and overrun key installations. Rebel leaders answer their Kuwaiti brethren from the island's radio stations. Because of the widespread support for the fundamentalists among the Bahrainian people, there is little resistance to their efforts. The revolution is all but complete.

KUWAIT INTERNATIONAL AIRPORT

The Gulf Cooperation Council

The history of the Middle East is replete with regional alliances and combinations which shift and change as circumstances dictate, with the main and sometimes only item of agreement being the mutual enemy – Israel, and the mutual target – her elimination. The Gulf Cooperation Council (GCC) is a new kind of alliance in the Mid-East, its aims being the defense of the area against external threats of invasion as well as internal rebellion.

The two major threats to the Gulf states are Iran and the USSR. The revolution in Iran and the continuing war between Iran and Iraq, with the direct threat to Kuwait in the 1982 'Ramadan' operation (when Khomeini could easily have blocked the main road between Iraq and Kuwait) impelled the GCC to examine its military options for defense. The parties involved (Oman, Kuwait, Saudi Arabia, Qatar, Bahrain and the UAE) began true military cooperation only after the Iranian air attack on Kuwait, in October 1983.

The purpose of the GCC is to establish a local rapid response force, capable of defending the vital areas of the member nations; i.e., their capitals and industrial centers, and areas of important natural resources. This force will basically consist of the total military capability of all member countries, probably excluding some of the Saudi forces which are involved in conflicts on the country's southern borders. The GCC's primary goal is the integration of training methods and tactics to be used by the various forces. An upgrading of the air defense capability of all the neighboring countries will effectively overlap and result in better overall early warning. EW is especially problematic, as the Saudi AWACS aircraft are restricted to supplying information to Saudi Arabia only; EW information could be shared by the GCC only if and when special agreements are signed with the US.

The Iranian aircraft, after a 20-minute flight across the Gulf at wave top level, land on both of the parallel runways; their ramps are lowered and Mujahedin jump out even before the Hercules have come to a complete stop. The Iranians secure a perimeter around the facility. Four Kuwaiti Mirages arrive over the field; the pilots have been told that 'something' is going on down there. Two of the French-built fighters are immediately downed by shoulder-launched missiles carried by the rebels and Mujahedin. The remaining two Mirages flee.

GULF COOPERATION COUNCIL
HEADQUARTERS

Officials gathered in a conference room mull over the Kuwaiti representative's appraisal of the situation. An aide enters and passes a slip of paper to the chairman, who then informs the others that Bahrain has already fallen to the fundamentalists. The Bahrainian representative's face turns ashen. Council members look nervously around the conference table. Grandiose plans spoken of just minutes ago are forgotten, and each representative wonders if his country will be next. One of the members reminds the others of King Hussein's promises that Jordanian forces would come to their aid if called upon. The council takes a quick vote and the call for help goes out to the Hashemite kingdom.

RIYADH

The Saudis know a crisis when they see one, and inform the American ambassador that it has been a long time since they last hosted visiting US Air Force units.

SOUTH YEMEN

The first of the three battalions of South Yemeni and Libyan troops, who were secretly redeployed near the borders with Saudi Arabia and Oman after their joint exercise the previous month, are ordered north into Saudi territory. Exercise Friendship becomes Operation Jihad (Holy War).

An unholy alliance between the Islamic fundamentalism of Iran and the Marxism of South Yemen and

North Yemeni desert patrol on camels. The harsh desert conditions and lack of roads make the use of the traditional methods almost irreplacable.

The Jordanian-Palestinian relations were never perfect. Although the Jordanian army has many Palestinian soldiers, it did not prevent the Elite Jordanian units from carrying out a massive campaign against the PLO in 1970. The Palestinians in Jordan never forgot, and are considered an unstable element in this country. Photo shows a Jordanian Saladin armored car in the Irbid region, 1970.

Many US Special Forces Mobile Training Teams (MTT) are deployed in the Middle East, as well as in many other world trouble spots, assisting and training friendly forces. (seen here, in Honduras and Salvador). These troops can, at a moment's notice, become the spearhead of a 'low profile' US intervention.

US Special Forces instructors train Honduran soldiers in the use of anti-tank weapons.

The Jordanian elite commando forces are considered Jordan's best, and are manned only by the King's loyal Bedouines.

7 March

Libya, something possible only in the Middle East, bares its teeth. An experienced leader of the Iranian revolution manages the Shi'ite uprisings in the north while, in the south, an East German colonel and his group of DDR military advisors lead the Yemeni-Libyan force into Saudi Arabia to draw Saudi troops away from Shi'ite centers in the northeast.

AL KUWAIT
[early morning]

A Jordanian commando battalion comprising Bedouins and Palestinians arrives, having been authorized and deployed immediately after King Hussein received the GCC request on the evening of the 5th. The Jordanians find themselves in fierce street battles and take their first losses. They also discover that some of those they are fighting are in fact Palestinians sympathetic to the rebel cause. This causes dissention in the Jordanian-Palestinian ranks, and the battalion commander withdraws his unit from the city to hold the highway to the airport, hoping that distancing his men from the street fighting will maintain force unity.

0830 GMT

THE KUWAITI PARLIAMENT
[1130 hours]

Kuwaiti officials, still hostage in the besieged parliament building on the third day of street battles, hear of the Jordanian failure to restore order. They now realize that their very necks have been placed on the chopping block, and decide to take the unthinkable step. A messenger escapes the facility and makes his way to the American Embassy where he presents his country's request for help. The ambassador passes this on to

Washington, offering his own opinion that, while the Kuwaiti army appears to be hanging on, it would be worthwhile to send a show of force to Kuwait's shores.

0900 GMT

MACDILL AFB, FLORIDA
[0300 hours]

Central Command (CENTCOM) receives word of the Kuwaiti call for help and immediately places its rapid deployment-capable forces on high readiness status. The joint staffs assign various units to CENTCOM for a low-intensity conflict; the US wants to maintain a low profile and is reluctant to be seen as over-reacting to what appears to its civilian intelligence officials as a local matter.

0930 GMT

ARABIAN PENINSULA
[1230 hours]

Immediately available in the contingency area are over a hundred Special Forces soldiers assigned to help the armies of Saudi Arabia, Kuwait, Oman and North Yemen. These highly trained men are ordered to consolidate into their predesignated A-Teams and report their readiness.

FT. BENNING, GEORGIA
[0330 hours]

1/75 Ranger Battalion, always on alert, is ordered to prepare to move to an 'unknown destination' and is ready within two hours. 2/75 Ranger Battalion at Ft. Lewis, Washington, where it is 12:30 a.m., is ordered to stand by.

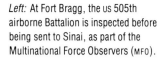

Left: At Fort Bragg, the US 505th airborne Battalion is inspected before being sent to Sinai, as part of the Multinational Force Observers (MFO).

A B-52 bomber, now part of the US Rapid Deployment capable Strategic Projection Force (SPF).

US troops instruct Sudanese soldiers in using the M-16 rifle during Bright Star exercise in Egypt and Sudan, 1983 *(left).* US paratrooper, 82nd Airborne *(right).*

1000 GMT

FT. BRAGG, NORTH CAROLINA
[0400 hours]

The 82nd Airborne Division is placed on special EDRE (Emergency Deployment Readiness Exercise) alert, and its battalion-size Division Ready Force (DRF) is given 18 hours to prepare for possible deployment. Its equipment has been prepacked at nearby Pope AFB. The lightly armed DRF is designed more to pacify a potentially dangerous situation with its mere presence than to quell any fighting. Should an actual conflict break out, the DRF would be backed up by the 82nd's Division Ready Brigade (DRB).

As the first DRF company steps aboard its transport aircraft, the next company takes its place on highest alert. When the DRF battalion's last company is called in, the next DRB battalion is designated DRF.

The 82nd's aviation components begin the long and complex preparation of their helicopters for deployment, and arc lights turn the early morning darkness into day.

SHAW AFB, SOUTH CAROLINA
[0400 hours]

Ninth Air Force headquarters, acting as CENTCOM's air power coordinator, faces a dilemma; its job in rapid deployment is to provide escort for military airlift and air support for ground forces. While the Ninth can prepare for escort duties while retaining the required low profile, its ground support responsibilities dictate its moving forces toward the contingency area. The deployment of powerful fighter-bombers would be anything but low profile.

The Ninth also had thrown in its lap the request made two days before by Saudi Arabia for a visit of USAF aircraft as a show of force. Reluctant to over-extend itself, headquarters decides to pass on the request directly, and not through the usual channels, to USAFE's 36th TFW at Bitburg Air Base in Germany, a location much closer to the contingency area.

SCOTT AFB, ILLINOIS
[0300 hours]

Military Airlift Command (MAC) headquarters receives notice to dispatch its aircraft for the possible airlift of alerted ground units, and mobilizes its forward command teams of controllers, maintenance people and security personnel.

LANGLEY AFB, VIRGINIA
[0400 hours]

The 1st Tactical Fighter Wing's F-15 Eagles move into high alert for escort duties. Conformal fuel tanks are added for possible long flights.

MINOT AFB, NORTH DAKOTA
[0205 hours]

Six B-52s and three KC-135 aerial tankers of the Strategic Projection Force's 57th Air Division are prepared for flight to their forward deployment base in Britain. The Stratofortresses will be able to loiter on station over the Indian Ocean, which will help maintain the low profile sought by CENTCOM while providing the means for quick ground support should it be needed.

U.S. NAVY HEADQUARTERS, WASHINGTON
[0600 hours]

Top naval commanders, groggy after being called in at 0400 hours, look with bleary eyes over maps of the contingency area. They are satisfied because, for the most part, battle groups are always present in key potential trouble spots around the world. Seventh Fleet groups are on station south of the Hormuz Straits, and a Marine Amphibious Unit (MAU) and its vessels are presently at Muscat. Another detachment of five

A KC-135 aerial refuelling tanker takes off at dawn to join the B-52s.

Right: A USAF B-52 prepared for a night mission.

US Air Force 1st TFW F-15A Eagle flying over its home base at Langley AFB, Virginia.

First light, an F-15A ready for take-off from its base at Langley.

---

ships, led by CENTCOM's forward command vessel, the *LaSalle*, is in the Gulf off the Saudi coast. A Sixth Fleet battle group, headed by the *New Jersey* and supported by another MAU, is presently on station off Lebanon and can easily be deployed to the contingency area through the Suez Canal. Two thousand miles to the south, prepositioned stocks aboard a fleet of ships off Diego Garcia can equip and support an additional

Marine force of brigade size. These groups and their support units are placed on highest alert status.

WHITE HOUSE, WASHINGTON
[0900-1300 hours]

During a tense meeting of the National Security Council, the president realizes he has been backed into a corner. In the past, the US had made it clear it would be ready to intervene at the behest of the Gulf states in case of a local contingency, but not in case of internal disorder. The CIA and military intelligence are at odds over the true nature of the problems in Kuwait and Bahrain. The CIA representative cites past occurrences of

internal disorder in the two Gulf nations which led to nothing more than quick and efficient reaction by local security forces. They are apparently unaware of the totality of the Bahrainian revolution. The man from military intelligence cites Iranian activity on the opposite shore of the Gulf, and reminds his listeners of the joint PDRY-Libyan exercise the month before. The defense secretary wants to move with caution – he

15

A KC-10A takes off from a civilian airfield to support the operation...

USAFE F-15s seen among the hardened shelters at Bitburg.

36TFW Bitburg based F-15s taking off from their West German airbase.

reminds the meeting's participants of US Marine casualties not long before in Beirut. His counterpart from the State Department then rhetorically asks what is the value of US promises if they cannot be backed up by action. The president locks eyes with his secretary of state, and, rising at his seat, says: 'We'll back up our promises. But let's do it without so much fanfare.'

1900 GMT

BITBURG AIR BASE, GERMANY
[2000 hours]

The aircrews of 12 F-15s belonging to the 525th TFS are assigned for the 'visit' to Saudi Arabia and are briefed on their flight route. Outside the hardened shelters, ground crew prepare the aircraft with conformal fuel tanks and defensive armament. At the nearby Rhine-Main AB, a KC-10 air refueling and cargo aircraft straightens out on the Frankfurt taxiway, loaded with JP-4 and heading for Bitburg to pick up the squadron's weapons, spares and maintenance crews.

1930 GMT

MACDILL AFB
[1330 hours]

With its orders received, CENTCOM designates its main command staff and orders it to air deploy to the Gulf and establish a forward command post. Until their arrival, actual forward command will be aboard the *LaSalle*, presently cruising with four other vessels in the Gulf.

The roll-on/roll-off ship USNS Mercury.

This is the base of the US Near-Term Prepositioned Force (NTPF), at Diego Garcia, where some 14 cargo ships loaded with weapons and supplies for an entire Marine brigade, are stationed at high readiness status.

The US Navy carrier task force 60, cruising off the Italian coast.

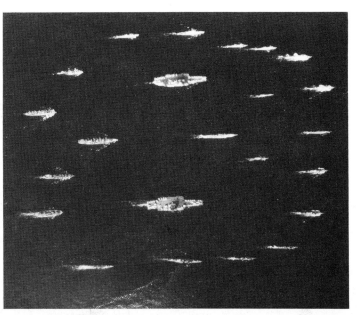

AT SEA
OFF THE OMANI COAST
[2235 hours]

Aboard the USS *America,* flagship of the Seventh Fleet's 77th Task Force, word is received of the White House decision. The vessel heads north at full steam; the task force commander orders the *LaSalle* and its escorts to go over to highest alert, and notifies his 8th MAU and its escorts, presently at anchor at Muscat, to move north as quickly as possible so as to be well north of the Straits of Hormuz before

any possible blockade is established. The *America* goes to battle stations, and a combat air patrol (CAP) of F-14s is launched to keep an eye on Hormuz airspace and is backed up by a flight of KA-6C aerial tankers.

OFF DIEGO GARCIA
[2240 hours]

Five ships of the 14-vessel Near-term Prepositioned Force (NTPF), carrying the equipment of the 7th Marine Amphibious Brigade based at Twentynine Palms, California, are ordered to move to a new location a day's voyage south of Oman. It will take the ships about three days to arrive on station and to be of any help to ground forces deployed in the area.

FT. CAMPBELL, KENTUCKY
[1500 hours]

The 101st Air-Assault Division activates its Division Ready Unit; the first-line troops, like their counterparts in the 82nd, will travel light. However, as much heavy equipment as possible, including many of the division's aviation group helicopters, is readied and will go with the first echelons. The commander knows that his only sure airlift will be with those aircraft already assigned the 101st; his idea is to 'get it out on

what you already have.' Arrangements are also made for the follow-up deployment of the group's heavy helicopters, which can be flown across the Atlantic on their own fuel, but need surface vessel support in case of emergency. Such self-flown deployments take about a week.

2230 GMT

TWENTYNINE PALMS, CALIFORNIA
[1330 hours]

Men of the 7th Marine Amphibious Brigade (MAB) are alerted and transported to Norton AFB, some 60 miles east of Los Angeles. There they will wait for C-141 aircraft to be assigned them. Their equipment is pre-positioned aboard the five NTPF vessels off Diego Garcia which were alerted almost three hours earlier.

2400 GMT

FT. BRAGG/POPE AFB
[1800 hours]

The 82nd Airborne Division reports a record EDRE time of 14 hours. The first elements of the division are ready to move, and wait for their orders. On the ramps, maintenance crews continue to prepare two of the division's Black Hawks; the commander has been told to go 'fast and light,' but he knows that his two choppers are worth spending a few more hours preparing so that he will have at least *some* mobility in the field.

At the last minute, the commander decides to include the DRF battalion's Echo Company tank-busting team; even if armor is not encountered right away, Echo's stand-off weapons could always be used against heavy vehicles and set installations, never mind explosive-laden suicide vehicles.

USAF 1st TFW Eagles in flight. Left, an F-15B being refuelled in flight, as seen from the KC-135.

The KC-10A flying tanker as seen from the Eagle's cockpit.

One of MAC's C-141B Starlifters in flight.

0200 GMT

0300 GMT

LANGLEY AFB
[1800 hours]

The 1st TFW reports that it is ready to provide escort. A flight of F-15s takes off for Torrejon AB in Spain where they will establish a forward operations base for escort duties between Europe and the contingency area.

EL GORAH, SINAI
[0200 hours]

The 82nd Division's 505th Battalion, deployed as part of the peacekeeping force between Egyptian and Israeli troops, is instructed to stand by for immediate transfer to the contingency zone. The US informs Cairo and Jerusalem of its intentions, and asks Egypt to supply air transport for the force. The Egyptians agree to the American request and say the aircraft will be ready to move by 'first light.'

HUNTER AIRFIELD, GEORGIA
[2000 hours – 7 March]

The 1/75 Ranger Battalion takes off in five C-141 Starlifters. To maintain the desired low profile, the aircraft head toward Europe, unescorted, on international air routes.

MINOT AFB
[1900 hours – 7 March]

Six 57th Air Division B-52Hs take off for England. Their apparently unhurried movement makes everything appear to be normal; little do people on the ground below the thundering giants realize that, this time, it's for real.

EL GORAH

[0700 hours and some time after first light]

The 505th Battalion waits next to its airstrip for the Egyptian aircraft promised by 'first light.'

Egypt now seems reluctant to openly help the US as tension is growing on its western border.

GHIRAN OASIS, SAUDI ARABIA

[0900 hours]

The first battalion of the joint South Yemeni-Libyan force arrives at this Rub al-Khali oasis after 36 hours of traversing some 100 miles of desert. A few palm trees hint at the water a few feet below the sands, and the vanguard force rests wearily against them. East German Army Col. Jurgen confers with the Bedouin Ahmed, a well-experienced tracker who is at home leading expeditionary forces as he is smuggling hashish.

The tracker tells the East German that the next oasis is only a few miles to the north at Naytal, where there is also a strategic junction. Col. Jurgen decides to take the site, and since word of intruders travels quickly in the desert, he immediately moves out one of his companies.

NAYTAL OASIS, SAUDI ARABIA

[1200 hours]

Three hours later, the company takes the junction after local Bedouin, some of them Saudi border guards, lay down their arms and offer their victors coffee. The vanguard is ordered to continue northward and capture Faris, the last oasis for another 100 empty miles. Col. Jurgen knows that whoever controls the water in the desert will win a war. Maintaining total communications silence, the East German then orders

US Marines take cover behind their Jeep in Beirut, while under Moslem fire from the nearby hills.

USAF E-3A Sentry AWACS aircraft being directed by a ground crew. Four of these aircraft are deployed in Saudi Arabia, supplying the Saudies with vital aerial surveillance and information.

Fanatic followers of the Ayatolla Khomeini cheer their leader as he arrives in Tehran. A new era is about to begin in the Persian Gulf.

a runner to inform the main battalion body following a few miles to the south to link up with the vanguard at Faris. Another runner is dispatched back to the assembly point in South Yemen to order the remaining two battalions to move forward. Riyadh is still in the dark over the invasion from the south.

HUFHUF, SAUDI ARABIA
[1200 hours]

During the day's third prayers, spiritual leaders in this predominantly Shi'ite city exhort their worshippers to rise up against what they call the Saudi regime's liberal policies. Unexpected support comes from Wahab tribesmen demonstrating in the holy cities of the Hijaz to the west. Simple weapons carried by the worshippers turn into Kalashnikov assault rifles and RPGs supplied by the PLO and wielded by young rebels.

Attacks are directed against National Guard bases, whose personnel have entered into the battle against the rioters. Rebels break into the military facilities and liberate heavier materiel such as machine guns and armored vehicles. Leaders whip the crowds to a frenzy, crying 'On to the oil fields.'

KING ABDUL AZZIZ AIR BASE, DHAHRAN, SAUDI ARABIA
[1200 hours]

Light weapons fire erupts around the perimeter of the Saudi air base to the south of the city where USAF AWACS early warning aircraft are deployed. The American commander is worried about the safety of his men and aircraft; half of his four-aircraft detachment is on patrol, and he orders his KC-135 to join them aloft, the airborne tanker being the key to his men remaining on station as long as possible. He also knows that a

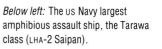

Left: USAF heaviest transport, MAC's C-5A Galaxy.

Below left: The US Navy largest amphibious assault ship, the Tarawa class (LHA-2 Saipan).

1000 GMT

1015 GMT

[1300 hours]

fully-loaded aircraft of this type would become a flaming pile of scrap metal from one well-placed hit by a rebel bullet. He orders the remaining two AWACS to remain on the run-up ramps of the two parallel north-south runways ready for takeoff.

The attackers advance closer to the air base perimeter and suddenly, appearing from nowhere, hoards of rebels converge on the installation's main gate just as the first fuel-starved foursome of Bitburg F-15s appears on a straight-in landing approach to the west-east runway. The gate is breached, and waves of attackers pour into the facility and are engaged by Saudi security forces. The commander orders his AWACS on to the runways and into the skies just as the first of the F-15s touches down on the perpendicular.

[1315 hours]

The first of the eight F-15s finishes a hasty and hot ground refueling from local F-15 facilities at the air base, taking on just enough kerosene to get to Riyadh, as all the base's hardened shelters are occupied by Saudi aircraft. It scrambles to the runway as Saudi security forces continue to pin down the rebels and buy time for the American jets. The remaining seven Eagles receive their last drops of fuel and, access panels still open, roll quickly to the runway.

Below: USAF E-3A AWACS aircraft stationed at Cairo West during Bright Star exercise, 1983. *Right:* AWACS in flight. *Bottom:* One of the radar operator's consoles inside the aircraft.

Soviet airborne troops ready for deployment. *Above:* Inside an IL-76 CANDID wide-body jet transport. *Right:* Loading an Mi-26 helicopter with BMD APCs.

BEIRUT
[1300 hours]

Radio Monte Carlo reports in its lunch-time bulletin that American fighter planes have landed in Saudi Arabia, and that US Navy ships are on their way to Kuwait. In the same bulletin, Libyan leader Qaddafi is quoted as saying that his country will 'lead the resistance against the Zionist-imperialist American-Egyptian-Saudi Arabian conspiracy.' The radio says Libyan troops have been put on high alert, and mentions reports of a similar alert in Egypt.

KIROVABAD, TRANSCAUCASUS, USSR
[1500 hours]

The 104th Guards Airborne Division, always on top alert, is ordered to prepare for paradrop, and boards AN-22 aircraft already loaded with equipment.

FERGONA AIR BASE, TURKESTAN, USSR
[1600 hours]

The 105th Guards Airborne Division is ordered to prepare for immediate deployment to an unknown destination, and its BMD armored vehicles are loaded on giant IL-76 CANDIDs.

EL GORAH
[1300 hours]

Men of the 505th are still waiting for the Egyptian aircraft promised by 'first light.' Egyptian liaison officers assure the commander that the planes are on their way.

1300 GMT	1400 GMT	1630 GMT	1900 GMT

RHINE-MAIN AIR BASE, GERMANY
[1400 hours]

The five C-141s with the 1/75 Rangers land at this American air base outside Frankfurt. The soldiers are ordered to remain inside the aircraft until dark to shield them from prying eyes on the observation decks of the sprawling international airport across the tarmac.

RAF MILDENHALL, ENGLAND
[1500 hours]

The six B-52Hs from Minot AFB land after an 11-hour flight from the US. A spot is cleared for them to park away from the usual place, something immediately picked up by amateur aircraft spotters. When questions are raised, the base commander personally answers them by saying the deployment is part of a SAC exercise planned some months previously.

EL GORAH
[1830 hours]

The 505th Sinai peace-keepers look up into the twilight sky in search of the Egyptian transports promised by 'first light' and promised once more for mid-day.

RHINE-MAIN AB
[2000 hours]

The Rangers of 1/75 disembark from the C-141s under the cover of darkness. A Ranger vanguard of two companies transfers their equipment to six waiting C-130s. The rest will follow in C-141s.

An SR-71 coming in to land after a reconnaissance flight.

The two crewmen of the Blackbird. Note their flight gear, almost like that of astronauts.

The MFO uses the former IAF base Eitam (now named Al Gorah) as its headquarters. The force relies on the French C-160 Transal aircraft, Italian light aircraft and New Zealand helicopters for aerial supply, liaison and patrol duties.

RAF ALCONBURY, ENGLAND
[2300 hours]
An SR-71 receives clearance to depart on a photo-recce mission over the Middle East. A side-flight has been ordered by military intelligence officers in Washington who have been wondering what happened to a joint South Yemeni-Libyan force that disappeared from view after an exercise a month previously.

SHARURA, SOUTH YEMEN
[0200 hours]
While Col. Jurgen's vanguard continues to push north, a pure Libyan commando battalion stages for heliborne deployment to As Sulayel on the far edge of the Rub al-Khali's sea of sand. The target is a small airfield which is to be used by attack aircraft supporting Jurgen's ground force in its northern thrust. Lt. Col. Mustapha checks the 20 Soviet-supplied MI-8 HIP and MI-24 HIND helicopters for the last time and retires to his command vehicle with confidence.

RHINE-MAIN AB
[0100 hours – 9 March]
The C-130s carrying the Ranger vanguard take off for a remote airfield somewhere in the Western Desert.

Right: KC-10A refuels an F-15 Eagle

Facing page, below left: US Marines dug in on Beirut's 'Black beach'.

Facing page, far right and above: USAF SAC operated 9th SRW SR-71 Blackbirds in flight.

Below right: US Marines assault a Spanish beach, during amphibious landing exercise, Crisex-81. The Marines come ashore with their LTVP-7s, in the background are their support ships; the Barnstable County, LST-1197 *(right)* and LHA-2 Saipan *(left)*.

Below: US Marines arriving at Beirut, 1982.

9 March

0100 GMT

FT. BRAGG
[1900 hours – 8 March]

The commander of the 82nd Airborne Division slams down his fist when he is informed that his 505th Battalion in Sinai is still waiting for the aircraft promised by the Egyptians. He decides to move his DRF, the 1/325 battalion.

Shortly after sunset, dark green C-141s dissapear into the skies carrying the first of the 82nd's battalions. Destination: a forward staging base 'somewhere in the Middle East.'

0130 GMT

LANGLEY AFB
[1930 hours – 8 March]

A second flight of F-15s takes off to rendezvous over the Atlantic with the C-141s airlifting the 82nd. These Eagles will pass off the Starlifters to the original flight of F-15s that took off from Langley the day before and are now waiting at the forward escort base at Torrejon.

0200 GMT

OFF THE KUWAITI COAST
[0500 hours]

The 8th MAU and its escorts arrive in Kuwaiti waters. An advance party lands at the port and moves into the city toward the American embassy. Reports from the ambassador in Kuwait have painted a picture of a situation under partial control, but the embassy staff have been locked in their fortress. The Marines entering the city discover to their horror that Al Kuwait has turned into Teheran, 1979, with rebels in just about complete control, and not a uniformed soldier in sight.

The advance party leader informs the task force commander of the situation, and suggests that MAU elements are landed to cordon off the embassy and evacuate its occupants. The commander informs Washington of the situation and awaits permission to move.

RUB AL-KHALI DESERT
[0600 hours; dawn]

Col. Jurgen has ordered his forces to move north. A force left behind at Naytal to guard the water sources will convey the East German's orders for the second battalion, a light, unarmored force, to move west as quickly as possible and link up with Lt. Col. Mustapha's heliborne troops at As Sulayel. The third battalion, the brigade's heaviest force, is to follow the lead battalion to the north. As Col. Jurgen's force moves out, one of his soldiers looks up and notes a white contrail in the lightening sky.

75,000 FEET ABOVE THE RUB AL-KHALI
[0600 hours]

SR-71 pilot Capt. Joersz turns northward on his run as Major Morgan, the recce systems officer, monitors his photographic and infrared sensing equipment. The infrared scanners indicate something suspect on the desert floor, and Major Morgan checks that his cameras are recording the details. The Blackbird heads toward the Hormuz Straits and Kuwait for further recce, and will hightail it back to the Akrotiri RAF base on Cyprus to develop its precious intelligence photos.

Below: The control room of the Amphibious Command Ship Blue Ridge (LCC-19). The ship can direct marine amphibious operations with its sophisticated command, control and communications facilities.

Below right: US Marines LTVPs come ashore, with helicopters hovering above — all part of a readiness exercise held by the USMC while on station in Beirut, 1983.

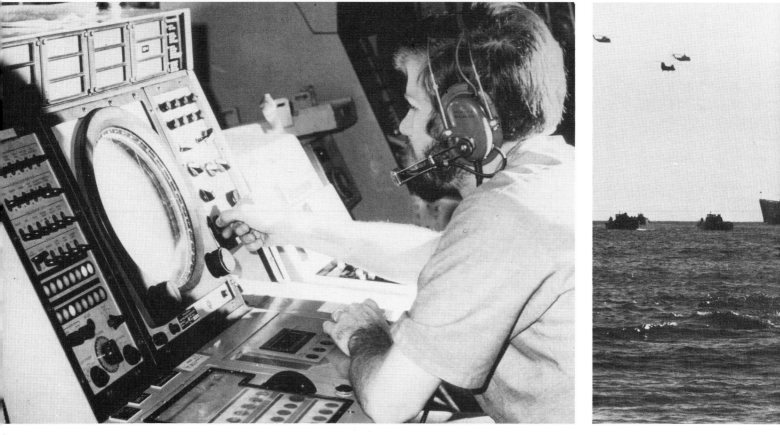

SOUTH OF THE HORMUZ AT 28,000 FEET
[0630 hours]

A US Navy E-2C Hawkeye picks up the radar blips of two large Iranian aircraft taking off from Bandar Abbas. The Iranian command has been watching Task Force 77 and its MAU heading northward toward the straits. The Hawkeye's data link relays its information to the air operations center aboard the *America,* which directs its CAP to intercept and escort.

100 MILES TO THE NORTH AT 10,000 FEET
[0635 hours]

The two F-14s of the *America*'s CAP make eye contact with two Iranian P-3F Orion maritime aircraft flying at 5,000 feet. They dive and join up on the Iranians' flanks. The flight leader, Lt. Morris, radios to the carrier that the Orions are heading directly for the straits and are descending to an even lower altitude. He is ordered to maintain formation, but not to make any aggressive moves unless the Iranian aircraft do.

The American-Iranian formation flies on toward the Hormuz which is just ahead, and descends even lower, to less than 1,000 feet. Lt. Morris watches the Orions intently; there is still no sign of irregular activity. The formation enters airspace over the straits, and Lt. Morris notices the belly doors of both Iranian aircraft beginning to open. He broadcasts a terse message to operations, which shoots back the order: 'Hit them.'

The first sea mines tumble out of the weapons bays of both Orions as the F-14s brake hard and turn into them, their cannons blazing. The first P-3F begins smoking and falls off on its left wing; it hits the water at a shallow angle and cartwheels end over end, throwing large chunks in all directions. The right wing of the second Orion is sheared off at the root, and the aircraft joins its mate in the Hormuz waters, disintegrating as it strikes the surface.

The US Navy ship Guadalcanal (LPH-7) seen on station off the Beirut coast supporting the 22nd MAU deployed on shore.

RH53 mine countermeasures helicopter taking part in a mine clearing exercise near Mallorca. Below is the US Navy minesweeper Illusive.

A Sea Sparrow ship mounted anti aircraft missile being fired.

0340 GMT

OFF THE KUWAITI COAST
[0640 hours]

Radar operators aboard the 8th MAU vessel and its escorts pick up unidentified airborne and seaborne targets. Gunners already nervously watching the shore for hostile movement are ordered to watch the seaward side for possible intruders.

Suddenly, a pair of Iranian Phantoms, their roar still behind them, enter into an offensive pass against the MAU LHA vessel. The lead aircraft is destroyed with a Sea Sparrow point defense missile and the second is downed closer in by a 20mm Phalanx battery. From port-left and below the Sea Sparrow's minimum intercept angle, two Cessna 172s cruise directly for the vessel. Deck hands wonder what pleasure aircraft are doing puttering around in the middle of a war zone. Loudspeakers blare the order to fire, and the point defense guns open up on the Cessnas with everything in their arsenals. One aircraft is immediately hit by the vessel's forward port Phalanx and crashes into the water. It explodes in a vicious geyser which indicates that these two pleasure aircraft are TNT-laden suicide planes flown by heaven-bound revolutionary guards. The second Cessna now draws everyone's fire; it is seen to emit a light puff of smoke from its engine, but manages to elude most of the hail of lead and crashes against the edge of the vessel's flight deck. A ball of fire marks the point of impact, but because the area is open, most of the damage is deflected upward and outward. The deck crews stare in horrific wonder.

A new warning is broadcast over the PA system: three small speedboats, overlooked during the confusion, are now bearing down on the ships from less than a thousand feet. This time officers and men open up on the intruders with their .45 automatics along with the rest of the flotilla's defenses, the most effective weapon now being the 76mm guns of the

29

USAF C-130H Hercules painted in brown desert camouflage lined up for take-off.

US paratrooper (note the T-10 parachute).

The Phalanx gun battery, an autonomous system using an on-board radar and independent fire control system. The gun is identical to the 20mm Vulcan gun used on many of the US aircraft.

escort ships. One of the speedboats blows up in a tremendous plume of water. A second begins zig-zagging, its crew apparently hit; the boat is found by a 76mm shell and explodes. The third continues through the withering fire straight for the LHA; at less than 25 feet out it is hit by one of the vessel's Phalanx batteries and detonates with a roar. Men of the 8th MAU flotilla begin to wonder just what kind of an enemy they are going up against.

0355 GMT

OFF THE OMANI COAST
[0655 hours]
The commander of Task Force 77 orders the five NTPF ships to head north in case the 7th MAB is called into the fray, which at this point looks like a major possibility.

0500 GMT

RAF BASE AKROTIRI, CYPRUS
[0700 hours]
Intelligence crews remove the films and data recorders from Capt. Joersz's SR-71 and rush them to the labs for development and analysis.

0530 GMT

WADI AL JANDALI, EGYPT
[0730 hours]
Six C-130 Hercules, their desert camouflage blending with the local colors, land at a dusty, remote airfield, and the Ranger vanguard disembark and stretch their legs. The Egyptian government had asked that the Americans not deploy to an airfield that had been previously used in Bright Star exercises. Half an hour later, the first C-141 lands with CENTCOM forward command communication equipment after a direct flight from MacDill AFB.

The Cairo West airfield, crowded with c-130 Hercules of all types and colors.

Target being hit by the Phalanx crashing into the sea.

An MFO soldier, member of the 82nd Airborne 505th battalion, dismounting from a truck on a Sinai desert patrol.

[1100 hours]
Incoming American traffic increases at Wadi al Jandali, and whole cities of tents appear in the warm late-morning sun. The six Hercules take off for Dhahran with the advance force of 1/75 Rangers, who are prepared for both air-land and air-drop deployment. Their mission is to maintain security at the King Abdul Azziz air base, which is to be used as the main ground base for the contingency.

EL GORAH
[1200 hours]
The 505th's commander is informed that Israel has offered the use of IAF Hercules to transport the unit to the east. The troops would have to arrive at the Hatzerim air base near Beersheba via ground transport, as Israeli military aircraft would not be allowed to land in the Sinai. The Israeli offer is accepted, and the commander orders his men on to battalion trucks with their personal equipment for the two-hour ride to Beersheba. Their heavy equipment can catch up with them later if needed.

KING ABDUL AZZIZ AIR BASE
[1400 hours]
The six c-130s land with the Ranger vanguard. The troops immediately establish security zones to prevent further attacks by rebels and their supporters.

Members of the 82nd Airborne hit the ground.

Hercules transports closely following each other in rapid take-off.

WADI AL JANDALI
[1430-1530 hours]
CENTCOM's forward intelligence detachment interprets the photos and data brought back by Capt. Joersz's SR-71. It is now realized that the scope of the crisis is far beyond what had been previously estimated. Washington is immediately informed of CENTCOM plans, and permission is granted for their undertaking.

1245 GMT

HATZERIM AIR BASE, BEERSHEBA
[1445 hours]
The first unmarked Israeli C-130 takes off with men from the 505th battalion. Destination: Dhahran.

1345 GMT

SOMEWHERE OVER WEST SAUDI ARABIA
[1645 hours]
The 82nd Airborne's 1/325 Battalion is ordered to jump over Ubayala oasis, some 50 miles from the northern-most enemy invasion force moving into Saudi Arabia from the south. They are ordered to establish defensive positions south of the oasis and prevent the enemy from taking the strategic site.

RAF MILDENHALL
[1445 hours]
SPF B-52Hs are ordered to prepare for a dawn bombing attack. Three aircraft are to take off as soon as they are ready in order to mount a patrol over the Ubayala DZ.

Paratroopers from the 82nd Airborne jumping from their c-130 Hercules.

Ready... Go!

1415 GMT

KING ABDUL AZZIZ AIR BASE
[1715 hours]
Ten unmarked Hercules land carrying the 505th Battalion. The troops join the 1/75 Rangers in preparing for base defense.

1430 GMT

OVER UBAYALA
[1730 hours]
The sky, red from the setting sun, becomes filled with silk as some 1000 82nd Division paratroopers and their equipment are dropped from the c-141s. Soldiers release themselves from their harnesses as soon as they hit the ground, regroup to check their status, and organize their personal equipment. The heavier equipment and initial supplies are readied for use, and after half an hour, the battalion is ready to move. Their helicopters and heaviest equipment will be landed at Dhahran.

1800 GMT

RAF MILDENHALL
[1900 hours]
The second flight of three b-52hs takes off to relieve the first flight of Stratofortresses which has been loitering on station over the 82nd Division's dz at Ubayala.

One of the 101st Air Assault Division AH-1 Cobra gunships being offloaded from a MAC C-5A.

FT. CAMPBELL
[0730 hours]

The 101st Air-Assault Division receives orders to move out to Dhahran. Twenty C-141s and 12 C-5A Galaxies will airlift the division's first elements along with more than 20 helicopters, artillery pieces, anti-tank weapons and initial support supplies.

MYRTLE BEACH AFB, SOUTH CAROLINA
[1200 hours]

Eight A-10 Thunderbolt II ground attack aircraft from the 354th TFW leave for Saudi Arabia. They carry their maximum load of fuel, but will have to be refueled twice before reaching their destination. Another eight A-10s stand by for deployment.

HILL 154, SOUTH OF UBAYALA
[0230 hours – 10 March]

The 1/325 is dispersed in its defensive positions around the narrow pass through which winds the only road northward. Taking advantage of the natural obstacles afforded by the deep sand and steep dunes, the men set up a textbook ambush. Light support weapons are positioned on the flanks, while mortar teams and the Echo Company tank-killers move to surrounding dunes.

TIME-OUT

At this point, large numbers of US forces are deployed or on their way to the Middle East. The Americans planned for a low-intensity deployment, but the discovery of the force moving northward in the Rub al-Khali desert changed all that.

The 8th Marine Amphibious Unit is now anchored offshore from Kuwait. It has secured the US Embassy and, to a small degree, has assisted Kuwaiti security forces in restoring some order. The situation remains

Right: C-141B drop heavy supplies to paratroopers on the ground. Normally, these are dropped before the paratroopers deploy to prevent injury on the ground.

Left: 354th TFW A-10s flying to their forward deployment base.

Left: At their forward operation location, fuel, ammunition and ordnance await the Thunderbolt's for their next mission.

Paratroopers from the 82nd 325th brigade building fortifications near their DZ.

serious but, for the time being, under control. The Iranian forces landed at Al Kuwait at the outbreak of hostilities have melted in with the remaining rebels and continue to make hit-and-run attacks.

The 7th Marine Amphibious Brigade is still awaiting orders to move out from Norton AFB on the US west coast.

At Dhahran are the 1/75 Rangers and 505th Battalion of the 82nd Airborne. Together they are providing base security for a massive US airlift, and the 505th is helping prepare the division's heavy equipment that was landed after the paradrop. In addition, CENTCOM's forward command post is being prepared for its staff, who are still at the staging base in Egypt.

The 82nd's 1/325 Battalion is preparing its ground positions after being dropped over Ubayala.

The first elements of the 101st Air-Assault Division are now airborne with their helicopters, and are expected to arrive in the contingency area late the next morning.

F-15s from Europe have remained at Riyadh after a hot landing during rebel attacks at Dhahran. Six SPF B-52Hs deployed to RAF Mildenhall in England are taking turns maintaining station over the area now controlled by the 82nd Division. A-10s have taken off for Dhahran from the US east coast. Four AWACS permanently stationed in Saudi Arabia continue to provide air surveillance.

Task Force 77 is maintaining station off the Omani coast and will stand by for the arrival of the 7th MAB. Aside from the 8th MAU flotilla off Kuwait, there is also a five-ship detachment, including the command ship *LaSalle*, stationed in the Gulf.

The South Yemeni-Libyan forces are advancing in two axes, one northward toward positions now held by the 82nd, and the other moving west to link up with a Libyan heliborne

Above: F-16s from the 9th TFW based in Korea being refuelled by a USAF KC-135 tanker, on their way for redeployment.

Left: SPF B-52 dropping a load of MK-82 500 lb high drag bombs on a low level pass over its target (Bright Star '82).

Right: 388th TFW F-16A taking off from a desert airbase in Egypt, Bright Star '82.

10 March

commando force. Its present position is 250 miles east of As Sulayel.

While the situation in Kuwait has calmed down somewhat, Saudi rebels are still battling government troops. The rebels have taken complete control of Bahrain, but, for now, this remains outside the sphere of action.

0130 GMT

50 MILES TO THE SOUTH OF HILL 154
[0430 hours]

A two-jeep patrol from the airborne force, using night vision devices, discovers Col. Jurgen's South Yemeni-Libyan vanguard moving north. They note that the enemy is led by two BRDM2 armored vehicles, followed by BTR60 armored troop carriers and jeeps; no heavy armor is seen. The patrol reports back to the command and is ordered to return to the main force by dawn.

0200 GMT

HILL AFB, UTAH
[1800 hours]

The first flight of eight F-16s from the 388th TFW takes off for Dhahran to augment the Bitburg F-15s in the air superiority role.

0330 GMT

35 MILES TO THE SOUTH OF HILL 154
[0630 hours]

Two of the three B-52Hs of the SPF on station above the general area are called in to bomb the vanguard of the lead South Yemeni-Libyan battalion. Coordinates are given by the 1/325 recce unit through battalion radio nets, and the giant aircraft lumber in at 2000 feet to drop their 100-plus iron bombs on the enemy formation. While the open and sandy desert does not provide the ricochets that account for much of the damage

Top: Paratroopers from the 1/325th brigade, 82nd Airborne assemble on the DZ right after the drop. (Exercise Gallant Eagle, 1982).
Above: Members of the 325th Brigade securing their DZ, Bright Star '82.

Assembling on the ground after the jump, the 325th troopers digging in using desert shrubs for cover and camouflage.

In the meantime, as more equipment arrives, Echo company assembles with their M-151A2 TOW jeeps.

A Libyan MiG-23, photographed by the US Navy fighters, in 1981.

caused by usual bombing missions, the results are nevertheless deadly. A lead BRDM2 is destroyed along with a number of BTR60s and jeeps. But it is the psychological value of a dawn bombing mission by two airborne behemoths at low altitude that affects the soldiers the most. Some are so shaken that they refuse to go on; they are threatened at gunpoint and ultimately decide on a few more minutes of life. Col. Jurgen knows the giant

aircraft were not Saudi Arabian – they had to be American. If the Americans were already in the game, he thought, the best he could hope to do would be to keep his force in one piece.

0345 GMT

MALAKA STRAITS, INDIAN OCEAN
[0945 hours]

The Soviet carrier *Minsk,* escorted by a group of surface ships, passes through the narrow waterway heading west.

0400 GMT

AS SULAYEL
[0700 hours]

The Libyan commando force under Lt. Col. Mustapha is landed by MI-8 and -24 helicopters at a nearby desert airstrip on the western access road. The field is to be used by SU-22 and MiG-27 attack aircraft. It is close enough to reach Saudi units that might be launched against the attacking forces, but far enough from Saudi air bases from where counter attack might come. The commandos prepare a perimeter around the airstrip.

Members of the 101st Air Assault division arriving by c-141. Troops are combat ready, but devoid of vital helicopters and heavy equipment their mission capability is limited.

A c-130H Hercules coming in to land.

HILL 154
[0800 hours]

Assisted by specialist air defense gunners, they establish several SU/23 twin barrel gun and SA-7B missile launcher positions, and prepare the initial fuel and ammunition for the helicopters and fighters to follow. The remote base is in a relatively safe location, masked by rough terrain and a steep ridge. It is out of reach of the prowling AWACS cruising far to the north, and Saudi radars at the Taif and Khamis Mushayet air bases to the east.

The tracker Ahmed looks tense; he feels something is wrong in the area and tells Col. Jurgen to stop and send a scouting patrol out for a closer look. The East German wants to keep his pace and brushes the Bedouin aside. An explosion rocks the column and the remaining BRDM2 goes up in flames. The BTR60 next in line tries to back up and gets stuck off the road in deep sand; it is hit by a missile and, as its crew jumps out, automa-tic weapons open fire. There is general confusion as BTR60s and jeeps try to escape.

Col. Jurgen understands the situation and requests air support from his forward base and orders the force to withdraw and reorganize. He calls the artillery, tank and Katyusha units of the heavy battalion following him to open up on the hill. As his lead force pulls back, the first salvo comes in. It goes wide, but the next salvos zero-in on the Americans. Col. Jurgen knows that his ammunition is limited, so he orders the first heavy barrages to be followed by occasional fire just deadly enough to keep the enemy pinned down.

THE OTHER SIDE OF THE HILL

The ground commander of the 1/ 325th realizes that there are forces with the enemy which his scout unit did not see, and calls for air support. Dhahran informs him that no US aircraft have yet arrived which are immediately available, but promises that he will request support from Saudi F-5s based at Abdul Azziz. SPF liaison officers, listening in on the net, inform Dhahran that they have a B-52 on station which did not partici-

pate in the original bombing run.

Dhahran is soon back on the line to Hill 154 with the news that a Stratofortress will soon be paying another visit to the area, and that Saudi Freedom Fighters will be overhead within an hour. The 1/325th's commander informs his men that help is on the way and in the meantime to dig in as deeply as possible.

[0850 hours]

At an angle, the lone B-52 roars over the rear-most echelon of the South Yemeni-Libyan force and lets loose some 50 500 lb. iron bombs as close as possible to the trapped American force without hitting it. The attack is effective in that it temporarily silences Col. Jurgen's artillery and scatters his tanks, delaying any possible armored attack on the 1/ 325th.

KING ABDUL AZZIZ AIR BASE
[0930 hours]

The first elements of the 101st Air-Assault Division land at Dhahran. The soldiers immediately work at unloading their helicopters from the Galaxies.

E-3A Sentry AWACS on station over a desert area. Four such early warning aircraft constantly patrol the Saudi skies. However recent experiences demonstrated painful gaps as intruders entered Saudi airspace without being located.

The Soviet made SA-7 Strela (Grail) man-portable shoulder-fired anti-aircraft missile which is extremely effective against low flying aircraft.

0700 GMT

HILL 154
[1000 hours]

A flight of four Saudi F-5s peel off to attack the forces of Col. Jurgen, which are still firing on the airborne soldiers. Three are able to release their ordnance and pull out of their dives directly over the enemy; the fourth, on which the South Yemeni-Libyans have had time to draw a bead, is simultaneously hit by two SA-7s and explodes in a ball of flame. Col. Jurgen's force remains pinned down expecting further attacks, something that will at least keep his tanks away from the besieged Americans.

0800 GMT

AS SULAYEL
[1100 hours]

The first MiG-27 Flogger arrives at the expeditionary airfield from South Yemen. Ground crews immediately refuel the aircraft and check its armament. Another aircraft, a fighter version, lands and taxis for refueling. After 30 minutes, both aircraft are ready to go. The narrow strip hardly affords turning room, and much patience is needed to get the jets into the air.

KING ABDUL AZZIZ AIR BASE
[1100 hours]

The first A-10s from Myrtle Beach land. Their leader meets with the 82nd's intelligence officers to discuss the situation and is told of the plight on Hill 154. It is decided that the aircraft will be flown against the enemy force and will land at the forward-most highway landing strip available, some 170 miles north of Hill 154. There, a Hercules will be waiting for them with more fuel and ordnance and, if need be, the A-10s will fly another attack.

Above: c-130 Hercules landing at a short desert landing airstrip.

Left: Ground crew loading bombs on a wing pylon of Fairchild A-10A Thunderbolt II.

Right: c-5A Galaxy heavy transport aircraft rolling on the hot runway at Cairo West.

0825 GMT

OVER RIYADH
[1125 hours]
An unidentified blip appears on an AWACS radar screen. The operator immediately transmits his data to the Saudi air defense control center.

0835 GMT

KING ABDUL AZZIZ AIR BASE
[1135 hours]
Saudi air force Zulu Team F-15s are scrambled to intercept the two unidentified aircraft heading northeast over the central region. The Saudis head south on an intercept course relayed from the AWACS.

0840 GMT

OVER RIYADH
[1140 hours]
Inside the AWACS the controller team supervisor deciphers the bogies' target as the unidentified aircraft head directly for the American positions. He requests permission to scramble American F-15s at Riyadh which is closer to the area. Permission is granted.

0845 GMT

RIYADH AIR BASE
[1145 hours]
Two 525th TFW F-15s take off with full afterburner and head southeast at maximum climb.

c-130 Hercules drops heavy cargo using PLADS system.

Below: An 10A Thunderbolt II firing its GAU-8A, 30mm Gatling type Avenger gun.

An F-15 fighter pilot in his cockpit.

KING ABDUL AZZIZ AIR BASE
[1145 hours]

The first A-10s, now refueled and armed, take off to support the 1/325th on Hill 154.

0855 GMT

OVER THE DESERT
[1155 hours]

First visual contact is made with the bogies, which are Libyan MiGs. The American formation leader breaks right and sits on the tail of one of the Libyans just as the Saudi formation arrives from the north. The American fires a missile and the MiG spirals toward the ground. The second MiG breaks left trying to evade the second American Eagle and finds itself on a head-on pass over the lead Saudi fighter. The Libyan launches a missile which the Saudi pilot skillfully evades. The Saudi now closes his maneuver in a tight turn and finds himself in formation with one of the Americans. The 525th pilot reluctantly gives way to his Saudi 'host', who launches a deadly 'Niner Lima' which flies directly into the MiG's tail pipe.

0935 GMT

HILL 154
[1235 hours]

Just as the first of the now-attacking enemy tanks is hit by a TOW missile, the paratroopers of the 1/325th recognize the shriek of approaching Thunderbolts between the explosions of the enemy artillery shells. The A-10s begin to let loose with their GAU-8A tank buster cannon, and the South Yemeni-Libyan armor grinds to a halt. The Americans now begin firing their TOWs and Dragons in earnest. The A-10s come in for another

82nd Airborne division's vehicles are paradropped from c-130s Hercules using multi-parachute drop.

pass; one of the paratroopers claims that he can see grins on the faces of the low-flying pilots. Considering the situation, this is acceptable from the happy airborne soldiers, even though any grins on the faces of the A-10 pilots are under snug-fitting oxygen masks.

1400 GMT

RIYADH
[1700 hours]

F-16s from the 388th TFW arrive. The flight leader seeks out one of the Bitburg pilots not scrambled on the intercept mission, who tells him what it was like to refuel with howling mobs taking potshots at his Eagle.

1500 GMT

HILL 154
[1800 hours]

A lone Hercules aircraft appears from behind a ridge. From its open ramp, dark shapes are seen to exit from which blossom a series of parachutes. The 1/325th's men open the supply canisters and discover ammunition, supplies and rations.

1600 GMT

KING ABDUL AZZIZ AIR BASE
[1900 hours]

The lead 101st Air-Assault units are ready to move out, their helicopters ready for flight. They are assigned the job of securing the western access road and outflanking the South Yemeni battalions in that direction.

Enter the 101st!

Left: UH-60A Blackhawk helicopter is offloaded from a C-5A transporter.

Right: The 101st UH-60s in action, transporting the unit's equipment to the forward operation base.

Below: Elements of the 101st in fortified position, protected by Vulcan canon as UH-60 and Cobra helicopters arrive, hugging the ground.

NORTON AFB, CALIFORNIA
[0700 hours]

The 7th MAB is ordered to deploy to Oman, and C-141s begin moving its lead elements. As the large force requires more aircraft than the Air Force can spare, the Civil Reserve Air Fleet is called in. Those leathernecks who are lucky take the First-class seats; the rest settle down in Business and Economy.

OFF THE OMANI COAST
[1900 hours]

Task Force 77's commander orders the NTPF ships, with the MAB's prepositioned supplies, to land at Salalah on Oman's coast. He also decides to send in the task force's helicopter carrier for support.

2000 GMT

NEAR HILL 154
[2300 hours]

Col. Jurgen decides to extract his vanguard and battalion forces and move west toward his other two battalions; he realizes that he doesn't have a chance against the Americans and their air support.

0500 GMT

AL HILLAH, SAUDI ARABIA
[0800 hours]

The first elements of the 101st Air-Assault Division arrive at this desert village 80 miles south of Riyadh. They establish a forward deployment base, and prepare a landing strip parallel to the north-south road. A forward air control team brings in to a landing a Saudi air force Hercules carrying fuel, ammunition and supplies for the 101st. More troops follow during the next hours, and the once-deserted spot rapidly becomes a tent city.

One of the 101st air-Assault units at readiness for UH-60s helicopters to take them into action.

0700 GMT	0830 GMT	1200 GMT	1530 GMT

[1000 hours]

With the first group of Black Hawks and Cobras arriving at the forward base, the 101st's commander decides to move out. He leaves his deputy in charge of the base and goes with his vanguard, a composite helicopter unit of Cobras and Kiowa scouts, to Laylah, another village some 150 miles to the south.

LAYLAH, SAUDI ARABIA
[1130 hours]

Arriving at this small village, the 101st's helicopters are surrounded by surprised locals who have never seen such machines. They are friendly enough to offer coffee and cigarettes. The maintenance team immediately carries out its usual post-flight check, and commanders begin a tactical planning session where they discuss the coming night's activities.

HILL 154
[1500 hours]

Two days after they were dropped over the desert, the 1/325 is replaced by the 505th Battalion. Arriving by trucks from a forward base in Harad, the 505th is now heavily supported by Saudi National Guard equipment. The 1/325th heads out for a good night's sleep.

LAYLAH
[1830 hours]

As the new base is readied for action, elements of the 101st take off for a night patrol, the first in a series planned for that night. The strike force includes most of the 101st's Cobras and Black Hawks, as well as Chinooks. The forces will use the forward rearming and refueling area to be established at Ayn e'Ajaliyah, some 100 miles to the south.

45

Left: This CH-47D is the 101st heaviest chopper, capable of lifting a complete M-198 *(seen below)*, its ammunition and crew, in one sortie, or, as seen here, lifting six full inflatable fuel packs.

Below: A C-130 Hercules coming to a low LAPES cargo drop.

Right: US Marine crewmen in action on the USS Guam flight deck, waiting to service Cobra helicopters returning from a mission (off Grenada, 1983).

1630 GMT

AYN E'AJALIYAH, SAUDI ARABIA
[1930 hours]

It is already dark as the lead elements are landed some 250 yards off the road. Even with their superb night vision equipment, the pilots can hardly see the desert floor due to the dust raised by the rotor blades. Soon to follow are the Chinooks, each with three fuel packs slung under their fuselages. They approach the site, drop their cargo, and return for another sortie. A Hercules comes over, almost touching the ground at 10 feet; a parachute appears from its cargo bay and pulls out a pallet loaded with supplies and water packs. The goods are immediately carried away from the area allowing a second LAPES by another C-130.

1000 GMT

SALALAH, OMAN
[1300 hours]

The first 7th MAB elements arrive from the US west coast in their C-141s. CH-46 Sea Knight and CH-53 Sea Stallion helicopters from Task Force 77 transport the Marines inland to a desert staging ground where they will wait for orders to block the enemy supply route.

1400 GMT

AL DIKAKAH, SAUDI ARABIA
[1700 hours]

The first battalion of the 7th MAB arrives by CH-53E helicopters at the southern tip of the Rub al-Khali desert. They take up positions on the sand dunes surrounding the narrow caravan path. The Marine leader knows the importance of this stronghold; the bottleneck is the enemy's only supply line, and without it, it would be only a matter of days until the enemy force begins to starve.

On station in the northern Indian Ocean, USS Midway (CV-41) is seen here cruising at full steam.

A US Marine Corps CH-53 Stallion helicopter ready for take off from USS Guadalcanal.

1830 GMT

WESTERN RUB AL-KHALI
[2130 hours]

Col. Jurgen's convoy links up with his western-most element, a raiding force made up of a light motorized battalion crossing the desert to support the commandos at As Sulayel. After a short briefing, Col. Jurgen assigns himself to the lead formation and gives orders to move out.

1930 GMT

AL DIKAKAH
[2230 hours]

The Marine lookouts hear noise from a possible convoy coming from the southwest. They estimate the range at six miles and the force tenses in its positions.

2000 GMT

AS SULAYEL
[2300 hours]

The Libyan helicopter detachment receives a warning of enemy operations in the area. A formation of HIND's take off to link up with Col. Jurgen's forces.

2030 GMT

AL DIKAKAH
[2330 hours]

There is no sign of any convoy, but everyone can hear the trucks. The noise sounds as if the trucks had already rolled through the Marine positions. Then, some four miles to the south, the first truck appears over a hill. The Marines keep their heads down and wait for the enemy to get into effective range.

[2400 hours]

As the enemy supply convoy enters the Marine killing zone, the night sky turns into day with flares and light weapons fire. The lead enemy vehicle, a BRDM2, burns from a direct TOW hit and illuminates the rest of the targets. Soldiers run from the blazing vehicles; ammunition trucks blow up; fuel explodes in a blazing inferno.

IRQ ABU FAQAR, SAUDI ARABIA

[0100 hours – 13 March]

The first 101st helicopters arrive at this sand peak, the Kiowas carrying out a watch for enemy movements. The unit commander sets up the ambush; his men will attack the enemy on the slopes, their vehicles on the steep sand hills making then sitting ducks.

[0120 hours – 13 March]

The enemy arrives earlier than expected. Despite the total blackout, Cobra gunners and pilots have no problems identifying them with their starlight viewers. At 1300 yards they open fire, aiming at the forward elements with guns and rear guard with missiles. The aircrew are so intent on hitting their targets that they do not notice the HINDs rising up from in the back of the hills behind them. The MI-24s have been attracted to the light of explosions and identify the American force. Lacking any kind of defense, two of the Cobras are immediately hit and crash; the crew of one is killed and the other is captured. The remainder of the American force breaks contact and tries to evade the helicopter hunters. Two of the Cobras attempt to return the fire, but, lacking effective sights, they are unsuccessful.

Left: Lurking low behind enemy lines, these Cobra gunships seek for the enemy's weak spots, and will attack when least expected.

Right: Soviet Mi-24 HIND gunships, though larger and more powerful than the US Cobras, they are heavier and less maneuverable.

Right: US Rangers guard detainees at Grenada's Salinas airport, 1983. The Rangers will spearhead any US involvement in any part of the world, including Southwest Asia.

Left: 101st trooper in action, using an M-60 7.62 machine-gun.

13 March

2330 GMT

[0230 hours – 13 March]

Col. Jurgen feels relieved that the HINDs are with him. With the captured American crew, he can begin to understand the level of US involvement and he orders his force to stop for a few hours to allow him an effective interrogation.

0030 GMT

AYN E'AJALIYAH
[0330 hours]

Having gained valuable information despite an unsuccessful helicopter ambush, a raiding party is assembled at the 101st's forward base. The party includes a platoon of infantrymen carried by a flight of six Black Hawks, supported by four Cobras. The H-hour is set at 0430 local time. The objective is the enemy headquarters, located by the force's scouts at Irq Bani Humran, an easy-to-miss place some 30 miles from the ambush site. Their faces painted black, the air-assault team is on its way.

0127 GMT

IRQ BANI HUMRAN
[0427 hours]

Only dim trails of light escape the heavy cloth over Col. Jurgen's tent, raised between his command vehicle and a truck. Inside, the captured pilots, though treated fairly, are pressed for valuable information. Then, a strange humming noise is heard and the dark night erupts. The Cobras fire grenades at the center of the camp. A HIND is hit and bursts into flames. Under the curtain of fire and dust blown about by rotor

Above: The heavy forces arrive. Only after a week, can CENTCOM planners expect substantial mechanized forces to deploy to Southwest Asia, using the prepositioned supplies located at Diego Garcia. The US forces frequently train the use of sealift in their exercises, here, during Big-Pine II in Honduras, 1983.

Vehicles and supplies being loaded on the USS Mercury, assigned to join the NTPF at Diego Garcia in the Indian Ocean.

blades, the American raiders assault the frantic guards who fire in every direction but the correct one. The 101st team leaders, equipped with night vision devices, assign their new targets. As they begin firing at the tent, a tall man is seen escaping. In the light of the blazing equipment, they can see his blond hair and Slavic features. They shoot at his shadow, and he suddenly raises his hands crying out: 'Don't shoot...!'

0400 GMT
_____

OFF THE OMANI COAST
[0700 hours]

As the vanguard of the NTPF arrives at this tiny port, tanks, APCs and other heavy equipment are off-loaded to be transported to the MAB. The port, guarded by Marines and Omani troops, is full of feverish activity.

0430 GMT
_____

THE PENTAGON
[2230 hours – 12 March]

The duty officer receives a phone call from his counterpart at CIA headquarters. He is told that information is coming in of Soviet airborne troops and transport aircraft being cleared for immediate takeoff from the Baku region in the southern USSR. Satellite information is received with alarming photos of new MiG-31 fighters staging at The Herat air base in western Afghanistan. ELINT analysis is flowing in with reports on Soviet deployments of large transport helicopter formations at Zarani, Afghanistan. The duty officer reaches for his red phone...

THE HEAVY FORMATIONS ARRIVE:
Above: An LCU brings marines and a supporting M-60 tank ashore.

The LCU lowering its ramp enabling the marines to scramble ashore.

Partly submerged the M-60 wades through the shallow surf towards the beach.

Evolution of the U.S. Rapid Deployment Forces

The C-5A is the USAF's largest transport aircraft. It can lift outsized cargo of many types; however, it is limited to airland operations.

Facing page, above: C-5A refuelled by a KC-10A. Long range airlift is one of the most important factors in rapid deployment today.

Facing page, below: C-141A Starlifter. This is one of the old A models. Since this photo was taken, all A models were modified, stretched to B standards and equipped for air refuelling.

Heliborne operations are still carried out with these Vietnam veteran Chinook helicopters. The latest version of the CH-47 is the Delta model, capable of heavier lift and longer range.

Rapid deployment capability for protection of American interests abroad was always one of the primary goals of United States defense policy. Previous ideas of force projection did not dictate the need for rapid deployment, but only the deployability of forces. Given adequate alert, America's available assets could eventually have been transferred anywhere, at least in a peaceful environment. Only when a realistic approach to force projection was considered was the need for time-phased deployment discussed.

Because the Soviet Union was perceived as the main threat to US interests after World War II, Europe and the Far East were considered the high risk environments, and thus American troops were pre-positioned there. Countering the Soviet threat at sea was less important as the Soviets had no significant naval power until the late 1960s. With total naval superiority and troops already in the 'hot zones', the US had complete control.

During the 1970s, several world developments dictated the need for a change in this policy. While having much of their forces assigned to the defense of Europe and the Far East, the West, and particulary the US as the leader of the free world, had no available forces, or even doctrine, to protect allies and interests in remote locations.

As far back as the early 1960s, US Defense Secretary Robert McNamara suggested a global intervention force of a fire brigade capable of deployment worldwide with the new C-5A Galaxy transports. But by the 1970s, this intention, in retrospect of the Vietnam war, was the last thing the administration wanted to hear about, and the concept was dropped. With no determined policy the US, often regarded as world's policeman, watched friendly governments collapse one by one under the growing pressure of terrorism, subversion and revolution, in almost every case with the inspiration, assistance and guidance of Soviet surrogates or allies, or terrorist organizations linked with the Communist bloc.

The US Marines are stationed afloat near most of the world's troublespots. They can reach any point on the globe within a few days, but with only a small force, like this amphibious, heliborne force, training in Turkey. For larger forces, the US requires its airborne troops.

Facing page, above: These USMC M-60 tanks assault a beach in Thailand during an exercise in 1983.

Facing page: The Marines are also practicing annual winter exercises in Norway. The 2nd Marine division (II FMF, Atlantic) is responsible for this area, as well as for the Mediterranean and the Caribbean.

The Marines undertake training in Chile.

The US Marines are the only force able to globally project heavy formations into a hostile area. This force is, however, too small to mean business...

Marines aviators and their aircraft in Somalia.

us Navy exercise in the Indian ocean.

us military aid, specifically in the form of weapons and assistance, would be offered or enhanced in order to gain a firm grip on the situation, but usually only after the trouble had begun.

Contributing to this trend was the fact that the British Empire had once dominated most of the world's vital spots, including in the Persian Gulf, Borneo and Africa. While us forces did exist that were capable of aiding such troubled small countries, Washington put little focus on these areas and their needs during the '60s. With the withdrawal of the UK from many strategic spots, mostly in Southwest Asia, half a decade's lapse of American involvement in the area left many nations under Soviet influence. The us counted on the Shah of Iran to be a stabilizer of his region, acting against aggression from Iraq and South Yemen and representing the West's interests in the area.

After more than a decade, with the growing threats to democracy and its allies worldwide, us President Jimmy Carter issued a Presidential directive to the military for it to start looking for forces capable of dealing with remote contingencies and supporting threatened us interests. The result was the Pentagon's proposition to create a pool of rapidly deployable, us-based forces to be controlled by the Joint Chiefs of Staff (JCS).

By August 1979, key units were identified among the various Army, Navy, Marine Corps and Air Force elements, and two months later the Rapid Deployment Force (RDF) was established.

Like the Shah himself, the us ignored the alarming signs of Islamic upheaval in the Middle East; Iran, driven by Carter's naive human rights policy, actually brought on the disaster itself. With the subversion by Islamic elements of the Shah's already well shaken throne, the collapse of the royal family was only a matter of time, and it came with a bang in 1979. As it became clear that Iran's collapse brought America's stabilizing efforts to an end, there was no counter-balancing force in

Other RDF units are those of the 82nd Airborne Division, which are maintained on 2 to 18 hours alert.

F-111Ds from 27 TFW seen over the pyramids, 1983.

Left: In order to solve heavy formations mobility problems, new light tanks like this RDF tank, equipped with M-32 76 mm high technology gun, were proposed.

UH-60A Blackhawk helicopters deployed to Egypt on board the Cygnus, Bright Star, 1983.

Left: The Strategic and Tactical Air Forces are participating in the RDF effort with two types of bombers, the B-52 and the F-111. Both are seen here taking part in Bright Star 83 exercise at Cairo West airbase, Egypt.

the area to stand up for Western interests. In 1980, the Soviets took advantage of the chaos and invaded Afghanistan, the first such military operation undertaken by the Soviet Union itself since WW II, excluding various police actions in their own Warsaw Pact backyard.

For such Soviet moves, the US had absolutely no answer. At the time, Washington did not have even one reliable ally in Southwest Asia, nor did it have any concrete defense agreements.

Most of the US airborne divisions, the only forces capable of rapid deployment to the Middle East/ Southwest Asian area, had been decommissioned after WW II and Korea; one division, the 82nd, survived the cuts and became the spearhead of US rapid deployment capability proposed by the 1979 study. The only other units available were the Special Forces and two Ranger battalions. But these alone did not necessarily guarantee success, as was determined by Operation Blue Light, the ill-fated attempt to rescue the American hostages being held at the US Embassy in Teheran.

The rescue attempt was the first undertaking by the new forces, which were obviously not yet adequately prepared for the job. While there was no question as to the personal skill and dedication of the personnel, the basic problem was, and always will be, force and operation management, task orientation and coordination. These areas, which will be discussed fully in this book, are always the pivot between success and failure. In the following years, US rapid deployment capability grew as coordination improved, operational routines were established and, in many exercises, the forces were trained to work in combined operations. While the US RDF offered no insurance against failure, it was indeed moving in the right direction.

In March 1980, a new unit was created in response to rising threats, the RDJTF (Rapid Deployment Joint Task Force). Capitalizing on the not-too-clearly defined assets of its predecessor, the RDJTF represented not

EDRE deployment exercises are carried out by all RDF capable units. The 24th Mechanized division began such a deployment at Ft. Stewart and Hunter airfield, where the unit's vehicles are stationed. The men prepare the vehicles, tanks, APCs, jeeps and trucks for the deployment and take them to the staging area at the port of Savannah *(Below)*, where the MSC freighter waits to load them. This time, it is the Comet *(Above)*. Note the rest of the equipment left on the docks. *Facing page, below:* The M-113s about to embark on the Comet.

The first operation to involve rapid deployment and operations in Southwest Asia was the aborted rescue operation in Iran. These are two of the RH-53 helicopters, specially painted for the job, seen here on the Nimitz' flight deck.

only a change in title, but also in responsibilities, as well as a first step on the road toward becoming a unified command.

Stationed at an ex-Strategic Air Command (SAC) bunker at MacDill AFB, Tampa, Florida, the new hybrid's defined missions ranged world-wide: to plan, jointly train, and be prepared to deploy and employ designated forces in response to contingencies threatening vital US interests (note the absence of specific target areas, specific forces, and means). In command of the unit was Marine Corps Lt. Gen. P. X. Kelley. In his first interview with the media after the announcement of the new task force, Kelley emphasized his unique authority to train, plan and execute operations, a first to be attempted in peacetime.

When the idea was first presented before the US Congress in 1980-81, there was much criticism raised over the force's capabilities and operability, and even over the new formation's authority to operate in its unnamed contingency areas. Some of the criticism was based on facts, others on feelings and emotions. Some congressmen called the new force 'a general with a filing cabinet.'

Since then, while rapid deployment force potential is still being questioned, Kelley and his replacement, Army Lt. Gen. Robert C. Kingston, proved they have at their command much more than just filing cabinets, with several large scale multinational exercises, the deployment of assigned forces to tension areas and the prepositioning of supplies and infrastructure preparations having been undertaken.

On 1 January 1983, the US Central Command (CENTCOM) was established, the primary mission of the four-service force being to deter aggression in its area of responsibility, Southwest Asia.

While not having a permanent land-based area of deployment such as in Korea or with NATO, the US Central Command relies on friendly foreign nations for at least temporary home bases. CENTCOM returns the favor by aiding these nations in self-defense and internal stabilization, as well as in overall regional defense.

As the US does not have enough strategic or tactical airlift capacity for a full scale deployment, the US planners rely on host nation support in command and control, infrastructure and air transport assets. *Facing page, above:* Saudi C-130 Hercules is seen during an airdrop. Use of such facilities and assets was frequently exercised during Bright Star. *Above:* The Egyptian Air Force base at Cairo West, after being 'taken over' by the USAF.

As can be easily understood, CENT-COM's day-to-day role is somewhat more politically oriented than militarily, despite the fact that politics and the professional military never mixed too well together.

Because a defense treaty such as NATO is hardly foreseen with the Middle East, all contacts are made through political channels by ambassadors and other diplomats. This is a limitation that could influence military operations; dependence on formal invitations, as so clearly outlined in the Gulf crisis taking place at the time of this writing, to intervene in case of emergency could impose severe restrictions on military planning, problems that for reasons of simplicity were not broached in our scenario. These could stem from such possibilities as the quick collapse of a friendly monarchy which precludes the issuing of a formal invitation; a communist revolution; or the legitimate election of a marxist government on a Gulf island followed by the Russians being 'invited' in, as happened in Afghanistan.

An answer to the question as to whether Washington will always wait for an invitation came from its Grenadian operation, where a determined move was based on a legitimate coalition of Caribbean nations who agreed to a US operation in order to defend themselves against possible 'fallout' from Grenada's marxist revolution. This approach, that of a collective invitation, appears to have been a step in the right direction that will allow the US to declare a red line beyond which each further step could bring about a military response.

FOCUS ON SOUTHWEST ASIA

Current programming for rapid deployment to Southwest Asia is based on two primary facts:
1) the stability and security of the region is vital to US national security interests, as well as to those of the free world; and
2) since a potential contingency in the area would encompass a wide range of demanding situations, programming for that theater provides the US defense establishment

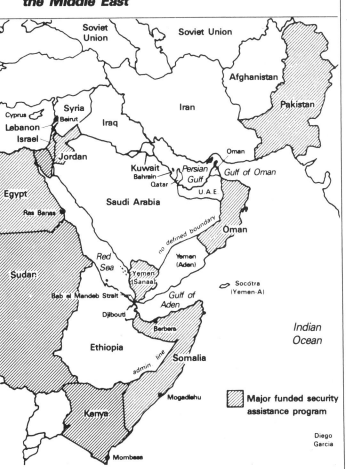

Southwest Asia and the Middle East

Major funded security assistance program

The Saipan (LHA-2) Tarawa class amphibious assault ship, part of the US Marine force positioned at some of the world's troublespots.

A Marine from the 24 MAU in Beirut. The soldier, member of the unit's target acquisition platoon, is equipped with night vision and high power binoculars to detect targets for the Marine's supporting Artillery.

with a robust capability which could cover the demands of other theaters as well.

The US sees the need to raise more units specializing in rapid deployment, but rather to adequately equip, prepare and train existing units for quick reaction and high readiness. In some cases, units designated for specific theaters are assigned rapid deployment status to help prepare them for the unexpected. While US deployment capability is aimed mainly toward Southwest Asia, it will thus benefit overall US military combat readiness.

What are the potential conflicts for which rapid deployment would be required? In general terms, conflicts which develop in those areas of little or no US presence are the ones most likely to demand rapid deployment. While there are many such locations, several key areas are highly important to US security. Each of these has its own special requirements, but it would be too costly to tailor a unique force to each locale. Therefore, priorities must be set. Flexible, mobile and rapidly deployed forces are now considered the most effective answer to the problem. Such high value areas are the Caribbean, where only a limited US presence is available; Africa, with no US forces at all, and Southwest Asia, which includes the Middle East, the Indian Ocean and parts of Africa. Other strategic points, such as the North-cap and the Mediterranean, are covered by NATO contingency planning, although such programs are not really effective enough to deter the enemy from undertaking a hostile act. Only Southwest Asia contains an impressive concentration of strategic assets while at present having no specific forces assigned for its defense.

For the last two decades, the Middle East has seen the rise of many anti-American movements, some inspired by the Soviets, others by extreme Islamic fundamentalists. The American allies among the Arab world are usually well-established, conservative regimes, fertile breeding grounds for revolution, with the

Using their new M-198 155mm guns in anger for the first time, the Marines achieved good scores on hostile targets east of Beirut.

While the forces in Beirut were facing combat, the war was simulated in Egypt during the bi-annual Bright Star exercise. An EAF MiG 21 and MiG 15UTI trainer join USAF F-16 and A-10 posing for a 'multinational training photo'.

Middle, right: The battleship *New Jersey* appeared in the Mid-East a short time after being recommissioned. The ship fired hundreds of rounds at Druze positions in Lebanon, but achieved questionable results.

Bottom, right: In the shade, but not less effective, are the undercover operations of CIA and Special Forces throughout the world, not excluding the Mid East. These MC-130Es, part of the USAF special Operations Wing, are based at Hurlburt AFB in Florida, flying support missions of personnel and equipment where needed.

The RDF forces must be prepared to fight in the desert as well as the central American jungle or the subarctic tundra, as most of the units carry multiple-assignment jobs into all corners of the globe.

Even today, Seapower is still the dominant factor in rapid deployment. Keeping strategic sealanes secure is the mission – a still vital worldwide commitment.

Surface combatants require logistical support for sustained action on the high seas – cargo and supply ships are an indispensable part of the task force.

Commanding a naval operation requires sophisticated command, control and communications equipment, which is now available on selected US ships.

one exception being Egypt. Due to such countries as Iran, South Yemen, Libya, Syria and Iraq, the Middle East has become a powder keg placed among the glowing embers of extremism and upheaval.

POTENTIAL CONFLICT INTENSITY

The US considers any conflict outside NATO as being totally different from the standard European scenario. Distant theaters, with minimal American presence or none at all, without adequate infrastructure and depending on long lines of support, and with extreme, demanding climatic conditions, are locales boasting elements which could only add to the enemy threat. This threat, however, is generally regarded as a 'low' or 'medium intensity threat' as compared to what is expected in Europe.

A typical example of the 'distant theater' is the Arabian Peninsula. Lacking substantial roadways and railroads and with only a few developed seaports, airfields and bases, a massive military operation could get into deep trouble if its planners are not adequately prepared for such shortcomings.

The first problem of military deployment to this area would be force mobility. Today, even a relatively small unit is heavily dependent on its support elements, its 'heavy tail'; forward elements can sustain themselves only for about 48 hours. The deployment of support forces is the main problem in RDF use. Support problems would begin as early as deployment of the forces themselves, as the US presently lacks sufficient airlift resources to carry even its single airborne division, never mind more. (While ships would be available, a sealift would be slow and cumbersome.) Overflight rights would not always be available, and, until recently, even air-refuelling capabilities were not up to numerical standards. Ground refuelling caused many a headache during the 1973 supply airlift to Israel, as many nations were unwilling to risk offending the Arabs by granting landing rights to Israel-bound aircraft.

The first solution to this problem

was to preposition material in probable contingency areas and thus cut deployment time considerably; this would mean that only the soldiers themselves would have to be flown in, while their weapons and supplies would already be in the general area. The only problem has been that local 'allies' do not view this from the same perspective as the US. Save for Israel, which the US refuses to include in the CENTCOM 'area of responsibility,' no Middle Eastern nation has openly agreed to allow the Americans to pre-position supplies on their territory. The US has there-

Above: The F-111 gives CENTCOM its only all-weather/night air attack capability.

Right: Berbera port in Somalia is only one of the improved facilities in Southwest Asia developed for future CENTCOM requirements.

Long range bombardment missions are the responsibility of the SPF's B-52s. (Below)

Within CENTCOM responsibility, Special Forces mobile training teams instruct Arab forces in use of US and Soviet weapons.

fore been limited to pre-positioning supply depots on the remote British island of Diego Garcia, the last British stronghold in the area.

Another problem for American rapid deployment has been to secure the long lines of transportation to the area, both sea and air, from hostile forces. While in the past no actual threat was considered, today, with Libya and Syria sitting near the main US routes to the Middle East, and with Iran on the other side, this problem could become a key issue. Sea and air terminals, which are few to non-existent in the Middle East, could pose another problem. Large

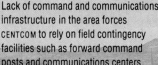

Lack of command and communications infrastructure in the area forces CENTCOM to rely on field contingency facilities such as forward command posts and communications centers.

amounts of funds for building or improving such facilities could end up wasted, with no guarantees that the Americans would be allowed to use them in time of emergency. (An example is the port of Berbera, which was developed by the Soviets but is now available for US use. The question is: for how long?) A better solution, but not as reliable, would be to establish agreements on equipment support by host nations. These agreements, although they might look fine on paper, would have to be considered only as a bonus; US self-supporting capability must be maintained to allow for any possible shortcoming. Therefore the need arises to have totally self-supported US forces with adequate means to sustain themselves for the period of deployment. In areas where host nations would agree to help support the American units, the forces would have to be tailored to the means of the specific host in terms of equipment compatibility.

The many types of scenarios which can be expected in the Middle East dictate the need for very flexible force structures and response methods, and the means for quick alert. The units allocated for such contingencies should therefore be streamlined to maximize their combat power immediately after deployment and in the initial crisis stages without unnecessary equipment. Training and preparedness levels also have to be continuously upgraded in respect to changing situations in the expected area of deployment.

Top: The Air National Guard A-7E Corsair is among several types of aircraft deployed for possible CENTCOM use. This specially painted aircraft belongs to the 138th ANG, based in Arizona.

Above: Among the many bases considered for US forward deployment is Cairo West airbase in Egypt, used severel times by US forces during Bright Star exercises. Masira airbase, Oman, recently improved by the US *(left)* is also frequently used.

Right: During Bright Star exercises the training forces have excellent chances to inspect and study foreign weapon systems, in this case a Soviet made Egyptian MiG-19, or a Somali MiG-21 *(Bottom left).*

Bottom right: During Bright Star, US Marines take part in landing exercises in the Red Sea and the Persian Gulf.

The command ship *La-Salle*, the flag ship of the US contingent in the Persian Gulf, was recently modified with communication equipment and with the Forward Command Element (FHE) on board, will serve as forward command base for CENTCOM in the area.

Intelligence and C³ in Southwest Asia

In order to control the massive air traffic during the exercise, Bright Star also trains the Air Force's forward command elements in multinational air traffic control. *Above:* Updating the sortie table. *Left:* EC-135 flying command post arriving at Cairo West. *Below:* A C-130 taking off. *Facing page, below right:* Egyptian and US officers at the control center.

Air transport is for fast response, but sealift is still indispensable for mass haul transport tasks. Each Bright Star sees the deployment of units with Military Sealift Command freighters. *Left:* Offloading equipment at Alexandria, using the ship's cranes.

Above: The Cygnus arriving at Alexandria with the 24th Mechanized vehicles. *Below left:* Heavy vehicles are off-loaded from the ship via the side ramp. The ship is a Roll on/Roll off design – specially suited for its task.

The Soviet Navy had recently deployed several new ships, some are already stationed in the Indian Ocean and Mediterranean. *Above*, the new Udaloy class destroyer. *Below:* The new Sovremniy class frigate. *Below right:* The new Slava missile cruiser.

The Soviet Kiev class carrier.

Below, left: The sa-8 gecko mobile SAM.

The Soviet Army has become more mobile with the fielding of new self propelled guns with its mechanized units.

As of 1984, the US had not yet redefined the threat in Southwest Asia as being anything other than direct, full-power, Soviet intervention. To quote Gen. Robert C. Kingston in his speech before the US Senate Armed Services Committee, 'Operating from southern Russia and Afghanistan, Soviet forces could conduct a ground assault on Iran to either seize the oil fields or secure their long standing goal of a warm water port.' While this view may or may not reflect an official US threat evaluation, the Gulf War and the spreading hostilities of the summer of 1984 proved to Americans that, while they may not immediately face the Soviets in Southwest Asia, they could be confronted by local powers such as Iran or Iraq, or a Soviet proxy in a contingency which would end up anyway with the Soviets in the Gulf. 'Clearly,' said Kingston, 'the most dangerous potential threat to the area is the Soviet Union.' The Soviets have increased both their indirect and direct capabilities to extend their global presence and apply pressure to local regimes. Indirectly, they use extensive military grants and sales, military advisors (over 8000 of which are stationed in the area, while there are questions as to exactly whom or what they are 'advising'), internal security personnel, and even combat forces provided by proxies such as Cuba. Their indirect capabilities include their ability to project power into the region with the recent modernization of their ground and air forces in the Transcaucasus and Turkestan military districts. With the expansion of the Gulf War, a new possibility must be considered. Not only could a Soviet-related threat get America involved, but so could a local conflict, and not necessarily one as widespread as the Gulf War.

To prepare for such unexpected events, the US must have a fully developed intelligence network in the area in question. This could be a problem, as the US began to set up its present intelligence infrastructure in Southwest Asia only in 1980, and making only a partial effort at that. Few details of American intelligence steps were mentioned by Gen.

Kingston in his speech other than the installation of an automated intelligence-related support system being installed in 1983 at CENTCOM's Mac-Dill AFB headquarters to quickly analyze the intelligence flow from the area.

With the lack of a fixed, forward-deployed headquarters, all American intelligence preparations must be done in the US, which is cumbersome and inefficient, but the best that can be done under the circumstances. 'Although providing initial progress toward resolving our intelligence shortfalls,' Gen. Kingston continued, 'we require additional essential capabilities in these areas, as well as other intelligence-related functional areas, such as human, imagery and signals intelligence.'

With growing pressure against the CIA in the 1970s, intelligence manpower was reduced and freedom of action curtailed worldwide. While all the agency's departments suffered, its Southwest Asia unit received a particularly heavy blow when its Iranian operations ceased. Both communications intelligence (COMINT) and human intelligence gathering efforts in the area have become much more complicated than before, as an agent insertion failure might cause severe complications in US relations with both its allies and enemies in the area. Spying has been somewhat limited to airborne efforts: SR-71 photo flights over the Middle East are frequently launched from RAF Akrotiri on Cyprus; data is continuously collected by AWACS aircraft deployed to Saudi Arabia; further intelligence is collected by USAF and USN electronic intelligence (ELINT) aircraft flying over the sea; US Navy P-3c Orions stationed in Diego Garcia and occasionally in Masirah, Oman, provide sea surveillance and ASW capability.

A step to get an intelligence grip on the area was taken in 1983 when a Forward Headquarters Element (FHE) was established on the command ship *La Salle*, stationed in the Persian Gulf. The vessel, a converted

The new generation of US communications satellites will greatly improve the intercontinental communications and add to CENTCOM's flexibility.

General Kingston, commander of CENTCOM, seen during one of his visits to Egypt during Bright Star. CENTCOM is responsible for all military contacts with the countries in its area. Some could have political bearing.

For global navigation capability, the US has developed the NAVSTAR system, consisting of 18 navigational aid satellites positioned in geostationary orbit. These systems will greatly improve performance of isolated forces deployed to remote regions.

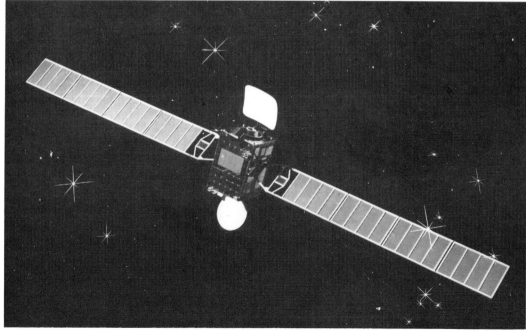

The new ARABSAT satellite system was designed to improve inter-Arab communications.

amphibious support ship, is equipped with communications and satellite links to Washington and maintains a forward detachment of CENT-COM commanders who provide liaison with allies and embassies ashore. In case of emergency, this facility may provide the only 'on line' operational command post during the initial phase of deployment.

The communications infrastructure in Southwest Asia is now undergoing changes, with the introduction of the first of a series of communications satellites (ARABSAT) which will upgrade present inter-Arab communications systems. This, however, is to be used by the local nations themselves and would not directly benefit the US except by providing more reliable open line communications in the general area. Tactical communications, both for inter- and intratheater uses, would have to be organized as the forces arrive. CENT-COM is seeking installations and infrastructure for theater communications in order to simplify the setting up of a full communication network for deployed forces. The organization of this infrastructure is not as simple as one might think, and a forward headquarters could prove to be unwise, as the location and deployment of would-be command posts have to be predetermined and linked between themselves and with other locations; as one can never be sure of the location of a potential crisis area, any pre-determination might result in CPs being far from the contingency. With the Middle East's traditional instability, such installations would also prove attractive targets for terrorists, and primary targets during revolutions or inter-Arab hostilities. They might, therefore, involve the US in inter-Arab wars much more easily then might be expected.

During the many yearly single service and joint US military maneuvers, communications networks are well tested, while outright communications exercises also contribute greatly to force readiness and interoperability.

The structure of US forces and their chains of command, while not being

In order to provide the deployed forces with adequate command and control, CENTCOM must establish a complicated and sophisticated forward based c^3 system.

Such advanced c^3 systems depend on satellite communications for both tactical and intercontinental communications.

Effective command facilities are vital for control of combat operations and secure logistical support.

For long range communications within the battle area, links between command posts may operate via mobile troposcatter radio systems, which are more reliable than HF radio.

exceptional, can seriously complicate c^3 during a Southwest Asian contingency. The forces may be deployed under CENTCOM, but they are each actually commanded by their own hierarchies. Army, Air Force, Marine and Navy units in fact multiply the total force's communications in terms of manpower (staff and maintenance), airlift sorties needed for equipment transfer, and paperwork. The Command's many links further add to the complications. A task-force set-up, with a commander responsible for all the forces through a single link and evenly-distributed command and control system, might solve such a problem. In the meantime, each force takes care of its own troops in matters independent of the operation, such as support, maintenance and personnel, while tactical decisions and planning for joint forces are done at the forward combined CP level. As for coordination on the tactical level, a new set-up, the Position Location Reporting System (PLRS), will identify the exact location of the system's carriers and will greatly improve force coordination and control, especially in dense battlefield conditions such as in amphibious landings or close air support operations.

Command and control on the battlefield is maintained through a tactical communications network which relies on high frequency (HF) radios, as long ranges and temperature degrade VHF/FM performance. HF radios, on the other hand, are not as reliable as FM in continuous communications – frequencies must be changed several times a day and according to atmospheric conditions in addition to the fact that they do not have reliable short range capability. As a solution, an airborne VHF/FM link or tactical communication satellite relay might be viable, but such things are not yet in service. Tactical COMSATS are operational as communications links between forward elements and the rear HQ and even CONUS, but do not solve theater communications problems as a whole. As for security and countermeasures in an electronic warfare environ-

The Quick Fix emitter locator heliborne system such as this UH-60 enables the intelligence battalion to intercept, locate or jam enemy electronic transmissions.

Facing page: The new PLRS systems now entering US Army service will improve the command and control capability by using an automated location reporting system, which reduces voice traffic and assists in location reporting during movement.

Unconventional warfare is part of intelligence gathering.

ment, the US would probably have an easy time in a low-intensity South-west Asian war despite some EW from Soviet ships off shore. But in a medium intensity conflict there might be problems, as most of the Arab armies are equipped with some kind of ELINT and EW equipment, though not as sophisticated as US countermeasures. New SINCGRAS (Single Channel Ground Airborne Radio System) vehicular units, which will soon enter service, will improve both security and ECM resistance of US communications, at least against those countermeasures now deployed in the Middle East.

Another issue is the interoperability of US forces with the military systems of host nations. Egypt, Jordan, Saudi Arabia, Kuwait, Oman, Sudan and Somalia are considered as being potential hosts, but only Egypt, Sudan and Oman have been willing to openly train alongside US forces, and, of the rest, only Somalia has allowed American troops to use just its territory. Egypt recently declared that it will not allow any foreign power to use its bases, including its naval facilities at Ras Banas. The military force structures of these nations are also not always consistent with those of the US. In many countries, American equipment is frequently mixed with Soviet, British, French, German and Chinese systems.

To test inter-allied communications, command level coordination and the use of host nation systems and support, joint RDF maneuvers are frequently mounted. Many of them are consolidated under the widely publicized 'Bright Star', in which the US holds four to five separate exercises in the Middle East to test specific contingency situations in simulations as realistic as possible. Three 'Bright Stars' have already been held, the first in 1980. It included elements from the 101st Air-Assault Division with their Black

Quick response to enemy fire and concentration of available firepower is enhanced by this Battery Computer System controlling artillery fire.

Electronics and sophisticated weapons are important; so is the adaptability of weapons to the deployment area. Compare the Egyptian aircraft's effective camouflage with the US Navy's...

Hawk and Cobra helicopters; elements of the 24th Mechanized Division with their heavy armor; and Special Forces and Rangers units. Air Force participation included F-4E Phantoms, A-7E Corsairs, as well as transport aircraft. Bright Star '82 saw the first deployment to Egypt of full units from the 82nd Airborne and the 24th Mechanized, and the first deployment of USAF Special Projection force (SPF) B-52s which flew in, bombed, and returned to CONUS non-stop. Bright Star '83 involved further elements from the 82nd and 24th, as well as tanks, APCs and SP guns, and joint Ranger-Egyptian army exercises with coordinated support by Egyptian and US aircraft. F-111s and B-52s flew in and deployed from the Cairo West airbase. Naval and

Marine units staged an amphibious landing in the area as well. At the same time, Rangers simulated unconventional warfare and held training exercises with the Sudanese army. The USAF also sent an AWACS from Cairo West to Sudan when tension in neighboring Chad grew due to Libyan involvement there. Marines staged landing maneuvers near the port of Berbera in Somalia and were supported by aircraft which later operated from a nearby base. A fourth exercise was held in Oman, with joint USAF-Omani air defense exercises and Special Forces training in Unconventional Warfare. The 1983 exercise included some 26,000 US personnel and 32,400 tons of equipment, and took place over a period of 20 days.

Above: In order to achieve maximum coordination with the ground forces, flexible planning is necessary. Here, an A-10 ground coordinator briefs infantry troops on the missions.

Below: Multinational training feeds new ideas and experiences into the system. Here, during Bright Star, Egyptian and US tank crews study the M-113.

Right: For the ground forces, adequate early warning is essential to prepare for an attack. Point defense radars such as this system are ideally suited for their task.

Desert Warfare

'A fortress to he who knows it and the grave to he who does not…'

This description of the desert environment clearly outlines its basic advantages and disadvantages. Traditionally, deserts were thought of as arid, barren lands, but in reality they are much more complex. They possess landscapes, climates and rich vegetation and wildlife known only to those familiar with them.

Deserts today make up some 20% of the Earth's land surface. There are two basic desert types: those created by climate and those resulting from topography. Both might look the same, but the conditions of living in them can vary. As examples, the deserts of Sahara, Arabia and Namibia evolved from lack of rainfall in their parallels. But the deserts of Persia, China, the US and Peru were created by the 'mountain rain shadow.'

Deserts have typical landforms, similar to those we know from other areas: plains, mountains and hills. The shapes of these desert landforms are, however, different.

Desert plains, either wide or confined to small intramountainous areas, offer the best mobility options for their worth. Made of large deposits of ablated rocks, or dry river beds, they are sometimes paved with a hard surface, while below that the material is soft and sandy. Dry lakes, salt lakes and marshes regularly appear in such places. While they offer perfectly smooth sites, excellent for a camp or airfield, dry lakes can become a deathtrap in a matter of hours. Some salt lakes are wet below the covering hard crust which can be broken by heavy trucks.

Generally, wadis and alluvial fans offer safe and easy access inland. Therefore, ambushes and kill zones can be installed using them as a lead-in element.

Sand is widely believed to make up most of the desert area, but in fact it is not so common. Vast sand 'seas' are located in the eastern Sahara and the Arabian Desert. Such sand deposits create unpassable barriers to vehicles and rarely does man dare traverse them. Special equipment such as light, highly mobile vehicles can drive in the dunes, but navigation and travel are difficult. Many sand deposits are shaped by winds, allowing easier passage along them.

Mountainous areas are separated from the desert plains by a rolling piedmont range. The piedmont, regularly made of rock deposits and in certain instances bare rock, is an excellent terrain for defenders. Mountain access routes of wadis entrenched in the piedmont can be fully controlled with vantage points on isolated mountains or high dry river banks. This is excellent helicopter country, both for assault and attack craft, which can hop from one hill to another, controlling wide areas with a minimum of troops.

On the other hand, areas of the piedmont can prove to be difficult terrain for mobile units, as tanks and wheeled vehicles are confined to specific routes which can be easily mapped and engaged by artillery or air attacks.

Mountainous areas are different from the rest of the desert. Desert mountains are regularly bare and rocky, and due to loose gravel, climbing is frequently hazardous. There are few accesses to motorized vehicles, and generally, footpaths are more numerous. In the high deserts, helicopter operations can be restricted by heat and elevation, also limiting this option. The most reliable mode of transportation in mountainous desert is the mule, horse, or camel.

Hammada plains are usually made up of a vast area of flat, high mountain surfaces. The rocky terrain offers good mobility for all vehicles; additional spare tires have to be taken along, due to high attrition.

Planetary deserts located in the 15° to 30° parallels are in the 'dry belt' of the globe. Due to the tropical conditions in the equatorial area, rain here is rare, almost non-existent. This results in large portions of the desert being plains, usually covered by sand, crusted rocks or riverbed sediments. The average rainfall of less than three inches yearly creates only a limited number of oases, most of them unreliable. Sudden rainstorms can surprise even the desert people – a whole year of rainfall can be delivered in a single torrential storm, while some droughts can last for tens of years. In some deserts, monsoon effects can bring very heavy summer rainfall. Mountain ranges in these areas usually receive more rain, and some of them even get occasional snowfall.

Due to the regularly clear sky, the amount of sun radiation is high and temperatures rise quickly. In the evening, temperatures stay warm and pleasant until midnight, while before dawn they can fall well below what one might expect from a desert area. The large temperature difference is crucial in the clothing of soldiers. In most subtropical deserts, summer is hot and subsistence is difficult.

Summer days can reach 130°F; winds are low and mirage visibility ranges to several miles at the most. In the winter, on the other hand, daytime temperatures are, to some extent, mild and pleasant, while the mercury may drop to as low as -25°F at night. The high winds, however, cause many dust storms, and torrential floods can inundate dry rivers.

At lower elevations in more humid areas, snow can sometimes be expected in the winter. This is mainly due to extremely cold nights and the absence of the compensating effect of vegetation. Snow rarely sticks on the ground, but icy nights can cause considerable problems to equipment that uses water for its operation. In the mountains, alpine conditions occur in winter. Storms can be ferocious and the effect of both ice and dust can be hazardous. Lack of preparedness in clothing, shelter and heat in alpine conditions is frequently fatal.

The surfaces of deserts located in parallels where rainfall is available may look dry, but under-surface water and springs or water pools in canyons can be frequent and easily accessible. This water, however, has to be carefully tested before drinking, as it can be too salty or tainted by minerals. Digging wells in riverbeds or in high watertable ground is possible, and frequently easy. In many streams, underwater seepage exists, while open water is absent. This occurs mainly in piedmonts and desert plains near the mountain legs. However, water in such areas is generally salty. Close to the sea, water is relatively close to the ground surface, several feet below. These areas are marked by extensive vegetation (palms, reeds). In deeper conditions, tracking of local wells must be done. In rocky riverbeds, water traps made of rock escarpments are sometimes covered by debris and sediment. Here, shallow wells (called t'mile in Arabic) can reach such water. Quantities available are limited and often already used up by local inhabitants. In sandy areas, water can be found only at oases. High deserts are generally richer in water deposits. While their plains have high salt concentrations, hidden valleys in mountainous and hilly areas regularly reveal springs, wells or t'miles.

Soviet Forces Deployment

Large-size Soviet intervention forces are predeployed at strategic locations and would be able to intervene effectively and at short notice in a Southwest Asian contingency.

The forces deployed in Afghanistan are ideally suited to render tactical air cover to operations in the Persian Gulf. Most important are the western Afghan airfields, which have had their infrastructure modernized to capacitate large combat air contingents. Lengthened runways and expanded maintenance facilities contribute to the feasibility of sustained air operations and the arrival of troops and equipment from the Soviet Union. Large-scale helicopter forces, already operating against Afghan guerrillas, could be assembled for heliborne operations, leapfrogging with air cover from forward bases on the Afghan-Iranian border to the Gulf combat area over desert staging points in a matter of hours.

As for airborne divisions and air-assault brigades, these are at constant readiness for rapid contingency plans. Capable of immediate deployment to the Persian Gulf are the Transcaucasus Military District's 104th Guards Airborne Division, deployed at Kirovabad, and the Turkestan Military District's 105th Guards Airborne Division, which has its regular base at Fergona. (The 105th is already deployed near Kabul in Afghanistan, and could easily redeploy to the Persian Gulf area if required.)

One should remember that during the Afghan invasion, airborne forces were flown straight from the Soviet Union. It should also be remembered that both the 106th Guards Airborne Division, based at Moscow, and the 102nd Guards Airborne Division,

based near Odessa, are both crack formations on high readiness status and could be deployed rapidly at short notice.

The Soviets have repeatedly mounted large-scale airmobile redeployment exercises in Eastern Europe and the Near East, climaxing with its massive operation to Ethiopia in 1977, where the equivalent of seven complete Soviet divisions were moved. Since then, the Soviet air transport capability has increased considerably.

Completing the Soviet rapid intervention capacity to the Persian Gulf is a strong naval force, with forward bases in the Indian Ocean. Able to operate with air cover from bases in South Yemen, the island of Socotra, and from Afghan air bases, Soviet forces could make amphibious landings at highly strategic spots, with reinforcements from airborne and heliborne units.

Land based air power operating around the clock could provide sufficient aerial cover for such operations, as well as take on American naval air power during critical stages.

Soviet YAK-36 Forger A STOL aircraft landing on the Kiev.

Soviet airborne troops on BMDs equipped with AT-5 SPIGOT ATGWs salute on a parade.

M-551 Sheridan tank, from the 82nd's Airborne Tank Battalion.

Ground Forces

Special Forces

In the aftermath of Vietnam, with US defense spending slashed to the bone, the American Special Forces reached their low point with the smallest number of operational groups since the 1950s. However, since the late '70s and the Soviet involvement in Afghanistan, the US had recognized the need for rapid force projection, covert operations, and the capability either to wage low-intensity wars or aid others in fighting them. The fall of Nicaragua, Angola, Ethiopia, Somalia (which later returned to the Western sphere), and Kampuchia, among others, all exemplify the determined Soviet effort to destabilize the Third World. Today, the US is regaining some of its tools for dealing with low-intensity crisis areas. The Special Forces, if properly used, may be the answer to the slow Soviet expansion in the Third World.

THE A-TEAM

Whether it's swimming, mountain climbing, traversing snow, moving undetected through the jungle, parachuting from airplanes or helicopters, or paddling a raft up an alligator-infested river, the A-Team is a complete unit.

This outfit is the point of the Special Forces sword. With only 12 men, its team of specialists can do almost anything, from blowing up a bridge to building a road or treating a sick child. The team was molded on the three-man OSS (Office of Strategic Services) unit that would be parachuted into occupied France during WWII to organize and supply resistance fighters.

In peacetime, the A-Teams have the skills necessary to train guerrilla forces of up to a battalion in size, or regular soldiers of friendly governments. The team is headed by a captain and lieutenant commanding 10 NCOs. Each is a specialist in at least one of the following skills:

1) Light/heavy weapons;
2) Communications;
3) Demolitions/engineering;
4) Medicine.

Most A-Team members are cross-trained in at least two skills—on a mission, they may be separated or killed, creating a void which others could easily fill. SF commanders come from regular units, retraining in the SF officer's course and taking the main course's five-week final test. After the officer's course, they take command of a team and coordinate SF elements with local (guerrilla or government) forces.

Rangers training in Korea. Three US Ranger battalions are assigned for short notice deployment missions.

The US Special Forces train in teams of 12 to operate as an independent, self sustained force.

For reaction in the face of low intensity/low profile conflicts, the American units in CENTCOM have access to the US Special Forces Command and its teams deployed in the contingency area. For planning, the head of CENTCOM has a full SF group assigned for Southwest Asian operations. However, a lack of preparation and personnel fluent in Arabic make it difficult to fully exploit this unit. The US Special Forces have traditionally been prepared for operations on a worldwide basis, with each team culturally and language-oriented to a specific area. Many SFers specialize in European languages, both eastern and western, and tongues of Southeast Asian and Central American regions. Today, emphasis is being put on the Arab world, and deficiencies should be corrected by the near future. The routine Middle East deployment of Special Forces would be as Mobile Training Teams, helping prepare Arab armies to operate weapons and mount simple tactics, as well as to learn specialized tasks such as freefall jumps, TOW missile operations and counter-insurgency warfare. Their deployment in the area would enable them to be called in during a 'no notice' emergency. It is unlikely, however, that these forces would operate in any other scenario, as the separate teams lack intelligence coordination and task-oriented training. Other US special forces available for CENTCOM use include two Ranger battalions and the Navy SEALs, with Special Boat Squadrons and Underwater Demolition Teams. All of these units can be supported by the Air Force's Special Operations Wing operating from Hulburt AFB, Florida, with its specially modified Hercules aircraft capable of the long range support of special operations.

A US Marines recce team.

US Special Forces: Stealth team operating in jungle country.

US Rangers on training.

M-551 Sheridan from the 4/68th Airborne Tank Battalion. Note the 152mm gun, smoke dischargers and IR tracker box above the gun.

XVIII Airborne Corps

US paratroopers manning an observation post in Grenada, 1983.

In charge of all airborne operations in the US Army is the XVIII Airborne Corps, with headquarters at Ft. Bragg, North Carolina. The Corps was activated in 1942 as the II Armored Corps, but received its blue airborne tab in August, 1944, when it assumed command of its first two units, the 82nd and 101st Airborne Divisions, which remain under XVIII Corps to this day. The divisions fought in Operation Market Garden (Arnhem, Holland) and crossed the Rhine. After a deactivation period of six years beginning in 1945, the XVIII Corps was reactivated for the Korean conflict, commanding the 11th, 82nd and 101st Airborne Divisions, as well as the 508th and 187th Airborne regimental combat teams. The corps served as headquarters for US forces during the 1966 American operations in the Dominican Republic, commanding the 82nd Airborne, the 4th Marine Brigade, the 7th Special Forces Group, and other support units. XVIII Corps was also in charge of the American operations in Grenada during late 1983, which saw the employment of Marine, Ranger and airborne units.

Today, the XVIII Corps is the Army's highest command in CENTCOM's rapid deployment forces, in charge of over 150,000 soldiers from the 82nd Airborne, the 101st Air-Assault, and the 24th Infantry (Mechanized) divisions, the 194th Armored and 197th Infantry brigades, as well as support units. The Corps has also been furnishing units from the two airborne formations to the multinational peacekeeping force (MFO) in the Sinai. Corps members, together with other Central Command officers, form the American 3rd Army, which becomes the headquarters in a CENTCOM contingency.

82nd Airborne Division

The 82nd Division is the only remnant of the large US airborne force from WW II. The division was activated as infantry in 1917 at Ft. Gordon, where it was discovered that there were men from each state of the union. It was then that the division gained its name 'All Americans' and its blue 'AA' shoulder patch. The division saw action in France in 1918, taking 7400 casualties in the Meuse-Argonne offensive alone.

After a long postwar deactivation, the division was reconstituted in 1942 and placed under the command of Gen. Omar N. Bradley. This time, it led the way as the US Army's first airborne division, jumping at Normandy in 1944. The 82nd returned to the US in 1946, and was kept active as a rapid intervention force. In 1965, a brigade of the 82nd was deployed to Santo Domingo, the strife-torn capital of the Dominican Republic, as part of the inter-American peace force. The brigade returned to its home at Ft. Bragg in 1966 after peace was restored. In 1968, during the Tet Offensive, the 82nd sent another brigade to the I Corps area of South Vietnam. The brigade was transferred south to the Saigon area and fought there for a time, returning to Ft. Bragg after 22 months in-country. The division was also the first to send units to the Sinai multinational force in 1982, and played a key role in Operation Urgent Fury on Grenada in 1983.

Today, the 82nd Airborne consists solely of airborne capable components that can be rapidly deployed to fight immediately upon their arrival at the contingency area. The 82nd is organized for both strategic and tactical deployment; its mission is to reach the target area as quickly as possible and sustain itself there for as long as needed.

The 82nd's basic fighting unit is the battalion, of which there are eight under the division's three brigades: the 505th, the 325th and the 508th. In addition, the 82nd has the US Army's only airborne armored battalion, the 4/68th, equipped with M551 Sheridan tanks. Artillery support is available at the battalion and brigade levels from the light M102 105mm howitzer, which is air-land and

A Dragon tank killer team in position.

heliborne capable. Other support units under divisional command are an air defense battalion, with Vulcan (now improved PIVAD) and Redeye/Stinger missiles, an engineering battalion, an intelligence battalion, a signal battalion, Division Support Command (DISCOM), a medical battalion, military police and others. A unique element in the 82nd is its aviation battalion, supporting the division with helicopters for transport, assault, reconnaissance, and attack.

Compared to the 82nd that fought during WW II, today's division has had its combat power multiplied

sevenfold. The list begins with personal weapons. While the paratrooper's traditional .45 pistol has been retained, the M1 rifle has been exchanged for the M16A1 (now being upgraded to M16A2) automatic assault rifle. This standard US Army rifle is a lightweight, magazine-fed 5.56mm weapon that is accurate and easy to operate.

Squad weapons are composed of the M203 grenade launcher and M60 machine gun. While the M203 is mounted on the M16 and firing 40mm AP grenades to 350 yards, the M60 is a modern 7.62mm belt-fed automatic weapon. Compared to the WW II-vintage bazooka and AT guns, the 82nd's present anti-tank

weapons are much more lightweight, agile, and lethal. The personal AT weapon replacing the bazooka is the LAW, now due to be replaced by a more sophisticated weapon. The LAW (M72A2) is a 66mm rocket equipped with a HEAT warhead. This is a 'fire and throw away' piece, with missile, sight, launcher and trigger mechanism kept very simple and cheap. The weapon can be quickly fired upon the sighting of the target, therefore exposing the infantryman for only a short time. Its range is effective at up to 300 yards. Its weight (2.36kg) enables the carrying of a large number of rockets with small units, and its lack of recoil enables a high hit

The I/TOW, now replacing the basic TOW anti-tank weapons.

probability of armor plates up to a foot thick. For close range, the optically-guided M47 Dragon missile is used. The expendable launcher, with the missile sealed in it ready for firing, can be easily carried by a single soldier as it weighs only 32 pounds. With a range of between 65 and 1000 yards, the M47 can destroy tanks in the small unit's area of responsibility. Each platoon has three Dragon operators, with each operator having an assistant; a total of nine missiles are thus available at platoon level.

Each brigade deploys a tank killer unit (Echo Company) that is equipped with the more sophisticated TOW ATGW. This weapon has a range of 3700 yards, but its 120 lb+ weight means that it must be mounted on a vehicle (M151 jeep) or fired from a tripod. Each Echo Company is equipped with 54 missile launchers. These weapons can be used against either enemy armor or bunkers. An additional support weapon is the 81mm mortar, operated by a crew of three. This short-range (under 5000 yard) weapon provides indirect fire sup-

port and is organic to the rifle company, with three per unit. The 81mm mortar can be broken down into three parts for back-packing, but is usually towed by M151 jeeps. A heavier weapon is the 4.2" mortar, which reaches a range of over 5600 yards with heavier rounds. These weapons are assigned to the battalion in a battery of four barrels.

Under divisional control, the 82nd has additional units which contribute to its power, mobility and support. The division's 321st Artillery Regiment includes 54 M102 howitzers providing direct close-in support (11,000 yards). The guns are operated in batteries of six per battalion, with 18 normally deployed in each brigade. Although obsolete, the M102 is the heaviest gun able to be paradropped. On the ground, it is usually towed by an M561 Gamma Goat six-wheeled vehicle.

The 4/68 Tank Battalion is the division's only armored formation. As the units do not deploy with armored fighting vehicles or personnel carriers, the only vehicles capable of

armored reconnaissance are the M551 Sheridan tanks of the 4/68th, the only US Army combat formation using Sheridans. The M551, developed in the '60s, is a light tank/armored reconnaissance vehicle, air-transportable by such aircraft as the C-130. The Sheridan is amphibious and has a crew of four; its main armament consists of a 152 mm gun firing HE rounds or Shillelagh AT missiles. The Shillelagh is a HEAT-armed missile weighing 59 lbs and capable of hitting a stationary target at 3000 yards. The missile uses infrared guidance and is not dependent on a wire like the TOW. Commander-operated M2 .50 cal and M73 7.62mm coaxial machine guns and eight grenade launchers are also mounted.

While the 82nd's stock-in-trade is airborne operation, it also has a significant airmobile capability. This is provided by the new UH-60A Black Hawk assault helicopter, of which 55 equip the division's aviation battalion. This helicopter is capable of transporting 11-22 soldiers at speeds of over 160kt. Sling loading

capabilities of up to 10,000lbs allow it to lift even the M102 howitzer. The Black Hawk is also used for MEDEVAC operations. The OH-58 scout helicopter is used for observation, recce, and command and control. It has a range of 260 miles, and can remain airborne for up to three hours. Scouting flights are usually performed by OH-58s armed with M27E1 Miniguns and 2000 rounds of ammunition. This additional weight limits its range to 230 miles.

The aviation battalion also includes AH-1S Cobra gunships, armed with TOW ATGW, rockets, guns or grenade launchers. The Cobra is highly agile and is capable of rapid mobility, forward deployment and rendering a flexible defense for paratroopers on the ground.

Air defense units of the 82nd are limited in deploying equipment movable by the division's air assets. The principal weapon is the Redeye, now being replaced by the new Stinger SAMS. A short-range (1+ mile), man-portable (26.5 lbs), heat-seeking weapon, the Redeye provides low

Mobile anti-tank team, an M-151A2 tow Jeep of 82nd Airborne Division in action.

A Sheridan crewman loading a Shilelagh missile on the tank.

altitude air defense. The Stinger has newer systems, mainly its infrared/ultraviolet seeker which enables head-on engagement, an improvement over the 'tail chasing' Redeye, as well as improved range. The second air defense system is the M167 Vulcan gun. It consists of a six barrel Gatling-type gun firing 3000 20mm rounds per minute. Its effective range is 1200 yards when used against aircraft, and 2200 yards when engaging ground targets. For anti-aircraft use the gun is slaved to an AN/VPS-2 radar set, itself having an effective range of 5000 yards. Forty-eight Vulcans are also used by the division's 4th Artillery Battalion.

Climate and terrain are major variables concerning the 82nd Airborne's readiness to deploy anywhere in the world on short notice. While under CENTCOM command, the division might deploy to Southwest Asia, but it may also be needed in the Caribbean, Far East, Europe, or, in short, anywhere. While training does give 82nd Airborne troopers important unit skills, extremes in both climate and terrain are not available at Fort Bragg. For this reason, the division's training program spans many off-post training segments. On many occasions, the 82nd is deployed in small units worldwide, training for all possible contingencies in Panamanian jungles, Alaskan tundra and Mojave Desert super heat and rough mountain terrain. Reforger in Europe, Bright Star in Egypt, and Big Pine in Honduras are only some of the exercises in which paratroopers recently took part. At their home base, the men carry out 230 days of extensive unit level and personal skill drills each year. Intensive physical training (PT) is conducted to keep the men in shape; during the year's training, the division runs a total of 10 million man-miles, makes over 100,000 individual parachute jumps during more than 120 mass parachute practice assaults in several drop zones around the base, and fires over three million rounds of all types of ammunition. Small unit training and other exercises emphasize night operations; almost 30% of the 82nd's exercises are held at night, with many drops made in the dark, enabling the force to be ready for battle at daybreak.

The climax of the on-post training program is the battalion-size combined arms live-fire exercise (CALFEX) conducted each year. During the CALFEX, paratroopers fight across several kilometers of simulated battlefield, firing live ammunition from personal and squad weapons and supported by artillery and air units in close proximity. Over 50% of the exercise's explosions are set off at minimum safety range, preparing the troops for the deafening roar, the blinding smoke and the choking smell of the battlefield.

The division's full strength is 16,000 men, of which almost 100% are airborne qualified. All of its combat equipment (including trucks, ammunition and medical supplies, in addition to the combat elements) can be paradropped into the battle zone.

NO-NOTICE ALERT
Due to various reasons, some obvious and others not so obvious, the whole 82nd Division cannot be fully deployed on a no-notice basis. To make the most of an available force at any given time, readiness procedures unique to the division have been developed. On a rotating basis, one infantry company and a few special support elements (forward artillery observer team, engineer squad and anti-aircraft unit) assemble all of their personnel, weapons and equipment, load their supplies and vehicles for paradrop, and stand by ready for deployment. This infantry company is called the Initial Ready Company (IRC) and would be the first element of the division to embark on air force aircraft stationed at Pope AFB, a Military Airlift Command base located at Fort Bragg. The IRC is the nucleus of the larger, more powerful, infantry battalion.

18 HOUR DEPARTURE
The infantry battalion is composed of three infantry companies, a combat support company and a headquarters company. When an infantry battalion is on call, it is referred to as Division Ready Force One (DRF-1) and is augmented with an artillery battery, an engineer platoon, bulldozer and water supply teams, a military police squad and a helicopter crew.

The largest force that is routinely placed on call is an infantry brigade. The brigade is composed of three infantry battalions and an Echo company tank killer unit. When the brigade is on-call it is referred to as the Division Ready Brigade (DRB) and is augmented with an engineer company, an artillery battalion, an air cavalry platoon, a military police platoon, a military intelligence detachment, and elements from medical, supply, maintenance and USAF forward air control personnel.

Several 'packages' can also be added to the various ready forces depending on the type of mission being undertaken. These include Vulcan guns, airfield construction units for airhead construction, air cavalry units with attack and scout helicopters, armor detachments, and civil affairs units.

Tests are regularly made of Emergency Deployment Readiness Exercise (EDRE) procedures, whose goal is 18 hours from first notice to 'wheels up'. Such exercises are regularly followed by three days of field exercises, in which the ready unit has to fight as is, which means only with the troops and equipment successfully organized for airlift within the allotted 18 hours.

SPECIAL AIRDROP TECHNIQUES
Only a few years ago, airborne units were regarded as obsolete in respect to modern military concepts. To some, the availability of helicopters, STOL aircraft and fast transportation made airborne concepts appear to be things of the past rather than the future. Dependence on weather, massive and continuous ground support, paradroppable cargo, and quick linkup with ground forces due to the necessarily small amount of supplies taken into the battle zone with the paratroopers, did not promise a glorious future for airborne units. But recent developments in the world arena, especially in Southwest Asia, and in parachute techniques enabling a modern airborne force to quickly deploy anywhere and anytime and to support itself for just about as long as it has to, have done away with the doubts.

Today, paradrop is possible almost anytime except in high winds. All airborne operations can be mounted without visual contact with the DZ. A new all-weather Air Delivery System (AWADS) is capable of precise navigation and safe delivery at night, in fog, or from above the clouds. MC-1B steerable parachutes are used in addition to the old T-10 models to enable limited air maneuverability while airborne. For control, the MC-1B has toggle lines and turn ports in place of some panels. As these parachutes are sensitive to different conditions, the more stable, but unsteerable T-10s are retained and used mainly for drops from C-141 Starlifter jets (which generate more air turbulence in flight) while MC-1Bs are used mainly with C-130s. An anti-inversion net modification was added to make the MC-1B more reliable.

A new parachute delivery technique is the Container Delivery System (CDS). With CDS, there is no longer the need to link up with ground forces for resupply. CDS allows equipment of various sizes and weights to be dropped from cargo planes under multiple cargo parachutes. Each such container is capable of carrying loads of up to 2205 lbs. A C-130 can carry 16 such containers, while a C-141 can carry 28. To drop their cargo, the aircraft fly at about 400 ft., pull up, and simultaneously release the containers, which exit the aircraft with their parachutes open.

When a very accurate degree of airdrop is required, several techniques using very low level flight and pinpoint extraction are employed. The Low Altitude Parachute Extraction System (LAPES) is a method utilizing a ring-slot parachute to extract palletized cargo from the rear ramps of transport aircraft flying at 10 ft. of altitude and decelerate it to a stop. Once over a predesignated spot, the pallet's parachutes are extracted into the airstream, and three seconds later the cargo is pulled from the aircraft. The total area length needed for the job is about 250 yards. Loads of 50,000 lbs have been LAPESed already, and the new C-17 will have LAPES capability for heavy armor as well.

Another accurate, low-level delivery method is the Parachute Low Altitude Delivery System (PLADS). This method can deliver loads of up to 2000 lbs within 100 ft. of a desired spot. It is similar to LAPES but differs mainly in the drop altitude, which is 200 ft. The pallet's horizontal velocity is near zero when it hits the ground, resulting in very little skidding.

When ground forces can prepare special facilities, the Ground Proximity Extraction System (GPES) can be used. With this method, the cargo is extracted by a hook which is released from the aircraft and catches a special arresting gear on the ground. There is no need for a parachute (the aircraft is flying at only five feet of altitude) and the cargo is braked by friction.

6th Cavalry (Air Combat) Brigade

The heavy helicopters are the transport element in airmobile units such as 6th Cavalry. CH-47 Chinooks are used for supply missions to forward units in the combat zone.

Among the forces designed to be rapidly deployed is the 6th Cavalry (Air Combat) Brigade. Taking advantage of helicopters, the brigade can fully exploit the third dimension for the location, disruption and destruction of the enemy's mechanized and armored formations. It can also support friendly forces.

Cavalry formations are, tradition-wise, among the richest in the US Army. The idea of cavalry dates back to 1866, when the 9th Cavalry Regiment was organized at Fort McKavett, Texas. The regiment took part in several actions there, pushing the frontier west and fighting Indians while defending the settlers. The 'Buffalo Soldiers', as the 9th Cavalry troopers came to be respectfully called by the Indians, won 14 Medals of Honor for their courageous and exceptional deeds.

After the Indian wars, the 9th fought in Cuba during the Spanish-American War where, with future president Teddy Roosevelt leading his Rough Riders, volunteer cavalry troopers took the impregnable fortress and hill positions at San Juan Hill. This battle won the regiment the crest with a five-sided block house figure, signifying the gallant battle for the fortress.

The 6th Cavalry Brigade itself was constituted in 1942 as a headquarters detachment for the 6th Tank Group and was sent to fight at Normandy during the June 1944 invasion of Europe, landing at Utah Beach. It later took part in campaigns ranging over northern France, the Ardennes and central Europe. The 6th was deactivated in 1945, remaining so until the formation of the air combat cavalry brigade in 1975.

The 6th Cavalry (Air Combat) is no less proud of its present forces than of its lineage. Formed in 1975 as a part of the TRICAP (Triple Capacity) concept, the 6th Cavalry was the second brigade formed in the 1st Cavalry Division. TRICAP called for the testing of a new cavalry division with three

The eyes and ears of the attack elements are these small and agile OH-58 Kiowas.

In Vietnam, armed Kiowas were used by the air cavalry for combat scout missions.

separate and distinct combat brigades: armored, air mobile, and air cavalry; as a result of this test, the 6th Cavalry was formed as the first, and only, air cavalry brigade in the US Army.

The brigade has two squadrons of helicopters: the 4th Squadron, 9th Cavalry; and the 7th Squadron, 17th Cavalry. (A third squadron, 1/6, is authorized at zero strength.) The brigade has a support element, the 34th Support Battalion; a signal element, 55th Signal Company; and an HQ troop.

The mainstays of the brigade are its two active squadrons, the 4/9th and the 7/17th, which have a mixture of four types of helicopters to fulfill air cavalry and attack roles.

For seeking out enemy positions there is the OH-58 Kiowa. While conducting this type of mission, the Kiowa normally flies no higher than 200 feet. It can achieve an operating height of up to 15,000 ft. and a flight duration of up to three hours with internal fuel. Both model A and C Kiowas are in service and teamed up with Cobra attack helicopters in what is known as 'two-three' and 'three-five' mixes. These configurations enable the enemy to be detected and immobilized with fast and effective teamwork.

The AH1s Cobra attack helicopters are the dominant factor in the 6th Cavalry. The highly modernized s-models are much improved over those which fought in Vietnam and are capable of performing most of today's missions, though lacking in adverse weather and night capabilities. At present, the Cobra's primary mission is the destruction of enemy armor for which they operate as a part of the combined-arms team.

For support of the fighting forces, two types of helicopters are used: the UH-1 Huey, for troop transport; and the CH-47 Chinook, for medium-lift transport.

To enable the brigade to fight effectively, the squadrons are usually given specific missions rather than support assignments for other troops. With their own 'piece of the action,' commanders can tailor forces and tactics to their own advantage, using terrain, deployment and other elements (defense suppression, etc.) as well as time. The forces are regularly deployed before dawn to a Forward Area Rearming and Refuelling Position (FARP). A fully-camouflaged FARP is established inside an enemy area and supplied with fuel and ammunition brought in by Chinooks. Attack and scout helicopters then come in, identify the location and surrounding area, and leave on their missions. After using all their ammunition or fuel, the teams can get back to the FARP, positioned only a few minutes' flight time from enemy positions, refuel and rearm, and get back into the fray. As there must be total communications silence, the pilots need to be excellent navigators to find the hidden FARP.

If located or threatened by enemy fire, the FARP can be relocated with just a few fast helicopter sorties. The attack formations can also continue to operate from additional FARPs which have been kept in reserve, or in long range sorties from the rear.

The new modernized AH-1s Cobra.

101st Air-Assault Division

The Apache helicopter, now entering the US Army, will greatly improve helicopter support capabilities.

The 101st Air-Assault Division was constituted on 23 July 1918 as part of the mobilization for WW I, only to be demobilized three years later with no combat record, having been too late for battle deployment. By August 1942, however, the division was an active airborne unit, with one parachute and two glider regiments, and on 6 June 1944, the 101st was baptized by fire at Normandy. After 30 days of combat, the 'Screaming Eagles' were sent back to England, returning to Europe in September for Operation Market Garden at Arnhem. Nineteen sixty-five marked the return of the 'Screaming Eagles' to the combat zone, landing at Cam Ranh Bay in South Vietnam. The 101st saw much action during the communist Tet offensive.

As dependency on helicopter operations in Vietnam grew, 'Air Mobile' was added to the 101st's designation, and it became the US Army's second such division. The first had been the 1st Cavalry (Air Mobile) which deployed to South Vietnam earlier. These were light, highly responsive units, with integral helicopter units and well trained troops. This change in names represented the shift from parachute to helicopter operations. The advantages in this change were fully exploited in the years that followed, as 'Air-Assault' replaced the 'Air Mobile' designation after new infantry-helicopter tactics were thoroughly tested at Ft. Campbell, Kentucky, and proven in several exercises, among them Gallant Shield 75 and Reforger. Today, the division's elements participate regularly in joint exercises, multinational training and MFO deployments, among others.

As the US Army's only Air-Assault division, the Screaming Eagles today are one of its largest divisions. It is a unique organization, using its helicopters to provide tactical mobility and flexibility on a scale never before realized. The combination of elite infantry and helicopters enables the division to engage the enemy so fast, and with such crushing firepower, that the mission of the army combat forces to 'close with the enemy and destroy him' might well have a divisional post script '...at 120 knots...'

The unique capabilities of the 101st Air-Assault Division are rendered from its flexible, combined elements. There are three brigade headquarters, each commanding three air-assault infantry battalions; an aviation group and an air cavalry squadron with three air cavalry troops; a divisional artillery regiment with three artillery battalions; and a divisional support command with the usual division-controlled support elements.

Naturally, the division's main fighting elements are the infantry units. These units consist of well trained and airborne-qualified men. The 101st's 1st, 2nd and 3rd brigades each consist of three battalions (each manned by 800 soldiers) and a headquarters company. The air-assault formations use the standard infantry weapons used by the 82nd Airborne and other infantry units. These soldiers, however, become air-assault qualified with a special course held at Fort Campbell, the Army's air-assault school.

The air-assault school is an effective introduction to those unique drills regularly needed for air-assault and helicopter-supported operations. Commanded by a captain and with only a few NCO instructors, the school introduces soldiers to the special techniques of helicopter deployment. There are assault drills from UH-60A, UH-1 and CH-47 helicopters, and courses in guiding the aircraft from the ground and loading and unloading them, including the use of sling carrying techniques which shorten the time helicopters spend on the ground to only a few seconds, therefore improving their survivability and availability in combat.

The school offers no less a physical challenge. Obstacle courses, some with dangerously high stations, identify those soldiers who might have trouble in airborne operations. The final stage qualifies the soldiers in conventional rappelling techniques which are used both day and night to descend from helicopters at

heights of up to 90 feet. Helicopter deployment standards have been improved threefold over previous levels by graduates from the air-assault school.

Supporting the air-assault brigades in combat are various helicopter units, all under the command of the 101st Aviation Group. The group's 101st and 158th Aviation Battalions are each equipped with 45 UH-60A Black Hawk assault helicopters in three companies of 15 aircraft each. Its 159th Aviation Battalion flies 48

CH-47A, B and D-model Chinooks in the heavy transport and mass-assault roles. The battalion also uses two UH-1 Hueys for command purposes. The 229th Attack Battalion combines a joint attack/patrol force of 60 UH-1s Cobra attack helicopters, 27 OH-58 Kiowa scouts and 13 UH-1 Hueys for command, control and supply. The 101st Group's headquarters unit comprises 10 Hueys and 10 OH-58 Kiowas.

The 101st Air-Assault Division has been characterized as the Army's 'all

purpose division,' a term suggesting its strategic and tactical flexibility and firepower. The strength of air-assault resides in the collective mobility provided by its organic helicopter units which contribute the capability to mass, disperse and recycle forces rapidly across the battlefield. The air-assault force is particularly well-suited for screening, covering and delaying operations, the reinforcing and economizing of force roles, rear area security moves and offensive operations into the

enemy's rear. These operations can be conducted in all types of terrain and atmospheric conditions, recognizing that periods of bad weather and reduced visibility enhance the concealment of flight routes as well as degrade enemy SAM capabilities. The division, using the vertical dimension, can with ease overcome obstacles which plague ground forces, such as rivers, towns and villages, and refugee and traffic congestion. Almost two of the division's nine infantry battalions can be lifted

Cobra gunships take off from a FARP for another mission.

Sling loading is extensively used by brigade to quickly move supplies and weapons in combat.

109

simultaneously by its aviation group. The rapid movement of these forces over long distances provides fresh assault troops for the fight, having eliminated arduous foot or motor marches to the battlefield. The division's howitzers, moved by helicopters flying 120kt at treetop level, add to the surprise effect and firepower available for the attack. Indirect fire can be massed on a target in an extremely short reaction time, with substantial combat power being concentrated at a given point on progressive reinforcement and supply, unmatched in speed by any other means. For example, the ground forces' 198 TOW launchers, each with six missiles, can be rapidly augmented by those of the division's Cobras. In an initial volley, ground launchers could fire just under 200 missiles while remaining beyond the enemy's effective range. With helicopter support, this number

could be multiplied many times. Practically speaking, such force concentrations are impossible, but this gives an idea of the division's capacity. A total of 366 M47 Dragon missiles are also available as anti-tank weapons, 36 of these weapons being deployed with each battalion's I Company in addition to the 22 TOW ground launchers of each D Company.

The 101st Division's capabilities grew as new flight tactics evolved and equipment was received. Exploiting the speed and stability of the Black Hawks and Cobras, the division's pilots were able to bring their aircraft down to very low level, 'nap of the earth' (NOE) flight, in which they do not exceed 150-200ft in altitude. Special night vision goggles aid the pilots in night NOE flights. Hugging the ground contours at 120kt may be frightening to the uninitiated, but it is rewarding in the long

run as it offers safer flights under combat conditions, as most of the enemy's defenses are incapable of detecting NOE movement, and weapons which can engage NOE flying targets, especially at night, are widely spread at tactical levels. Trees, cables, and houses are all flight hazards, not to mention hills and mountains. As both reading the instruments and looking outside is impossible, the workload has to be shared equally by the two-pilot crew. One monitors the gauges while the other flies, these duties being rotated every few minutes. Regular use of infrared markers and IR searchlights enable the crew to illuminate the LZ, any obstacles, or to search on the ground without being detected by the enemy.

The 101st Division thus moves by air and fights on the ground as a combined arms unit. It has well organized support elements, including integral

A Kiowa scout helicopter being ferried by MSC ship Ohio to take part in Gallant Eagle exercise in California.

Blackhawk helicopter deploys a Vulcan battery to a forward location.

intelligence and scout units. But this complicated network of forces needs a high level of coordination. Sustaining the force in battle is done by maintaining the momentum of the attack through the recycling of aviation assets and keeping lead forces fresh. Attack helicopters rearm at forward locations and, as a result, constantly support forces at the front. Because of its tactical efficiency and extraordinary firepower, the division rarely needs to provide for reserves in organizing for a given operation. As the battle develops, the need for tactical ground reserves would be met by the helicopter extraction of the most lightly engaged force and its redeployment in a critical area. This concept provides almost a 30% increase in available forces for planning purposes.

The division has perfected its air-assault doctrine to unprecedented levels. With unique command and control routines, the aviation, support and infantry elements have been carefully integrated to make the most of the available force. Scrapping the Vietnam era's cumbersome chain of command which hindered helicopter availability, the division's integral helicopter fleet insures a smoother flow.

The division's Combat Aviation Command Post (CACP) is the nerve center for its aviation operations. A high degree of coordination has been attained by the creation of the dedicated Combat Aviation Management (CAM) system, where command and control is represented at each of the division's levels. At the brigade level is the Combat Aviation Command Center (CACC), each with an aviation battalion commander, an S3 (operations officer), S2 (intelligence officer), a flight operations officer, a communications section and a weather team. This detachment of the aviation group is responsible for its 'interests' in all operational planning: to coordinate and execute combined missions and to solve, on the spot, any aviation-related problem arising at the brigade level. It is also responsible for directing brigade support. Under its command are two assault companies of Black Hawks; one attack company of Cobras; scout helicopters; a cavalry troop; a medium lift platoon of three Black Hawks, 10 Hueys and an OH-6A for liaison; the brigade aviation section; an air ambulance; and a pathfinder platoon. Pathfinders are expert infantrymen, paratroopers and scouts. In earlier days, pathfinders were the first to jump in order to mark the DZ for the rest of the force. Today, their job is retained, but in addition, they are now also experts in air-assault. All together there is a total of 75 helicopters, all under direct brigade command through its CACC. It is clear that the CACC's airspace management responsibilities alone are a lot of work, but the battlefield management of its assets such as support, rearming, refuelling and other logistical problems also come under the CACC's jurisdiction. Another problem it must face is enemy air defense. Its task in this case is to disseminate airspace, to suppress enemy fire before and during the operation, and to coordinate counterfire.

The lower level of CAM representation is the Combat Aviation Party (CAP), represented at each air-assault battalion command post. Here, a captain, a first lieutenant, a pathfinder section and a communications team provide the link between air and ground troops. The CAP coordinates all the battalion's aviation operations by determining available flight routes, selecting landing and pick-up zones, assigning the right helicopters for missions, and coordinating MEDEVAC flights.

At the company level, the CAM is represented by the Combat Aviation Team (CAT), with a sergeant in charge of coordinating company ground and air operations, as well as commanding the unit's pathfinders.

Although helicopters are important, the soldiers themselves are the ones who win the battles. Of these, the 101st has plenty, grouped in nine air-assault battalions. The typical brigade commands three battalions plus an artillery battalion and a 'slice' of all the division's units needed for the mission, such as air defense, engineering and signal. The division's support command (DISCOM) is responsible for sustaining the forces, leaving the fighting elements themselves relatively light and flexible.

Support for the fighting forces does not come solely from the air. Ground units are also available to support the fighting team and they, too, heavily depend on helicopters for effective deployment. For instance, the division's artillery regiment uses two types of guns. The 105mm M102, with its 11,000 yard range, weighs only 3,310 lbs and, along with its ammunition and crew, can be quickly relocated by one Black Hawk sortie. The regiment's heavier 155mm M198 howitzer can be transported by the latest Chinook model which can carry the gun, its ammunition and crew in one sortie, a total of 21,000 lbs, using its three-hook design.

The impressive capabilities of the 101st Air-Assault Division would be useless if it were not able to rapidly deploy to the battlefield. To accomplish this, the division depends on air force and naval assets. The division's infantrymen can easily be deployed by USAF MAC airlift or commercial airlines. The problems begin with the transportation of heavy vehicles, initial supplies, and, the most problematic, the division's helicopters. As the 101st is a high priority unit under the CENTCOM order of battle, it is allowed, for planning purposes, to use air transport facilities for a whole brigade, the other two being deployed by sea. While Ft. Campbell's airfield can support MAC aircraft, the two seagoing brigades will have to be transported over 500 miles to New Orleans for departure.

Airlift shortfalls will not prevent the 101st from being prepared. The division is regularly on the same alert status as the 82nd Airborne Division, with the EDRE 18-hour alert and an Initial Ready Company (IRC) on two-hour alert. The division prepares for a contingency according to the expected threat. A high intensity, NATO-type contingency would call for a massive deployment of anti-tank and air defense forces, while a low intensity, Grenada-class mission might need more light and light support weapons, as well as helicopters and medium-weight supplies. A Middle East-type contingency would require additional supplies to compensate for the lack of local infrastructure.

To solve the problems of oversized and outsized cargo, new equipment being considered for the division would be air-transportable by C-130 and C-141 aircraft with only a few items requiring the C-5 Galaxy. At present, a low intensity contingency would require a total of 186 MAC aircraft to transport the 101st Division in 'real time': 174 C-141s (50 of them for supplies) and 12 C-5s. The division could be fully deployed with 1111 sorties. Deployment preparations would have to take into account the time needed to prepare the division's helicopters. With sealift, only the rotors would have to be folded; airlifting the Black Hawk with a C-141 would not be so easy. The UH-60's tail and rotors would have to be folded, and the rotor mast removed, the whole process taking some four hours, with another four required to prepare the Black Hawk for flight at its destination. A C-141 can take 3 UH-60s, while a C-5 can accommodate six. The Galaxy would be needed more for the airlifting of the Chinooks, the heaviest, largest, and most difficult to prepare of the division's helicopters. The CH-47A and B models have over 1000 hydraulic pipe connectors to take apart to bring the Chinook down to a size accepted by the Galaxy, and at their destination the parts would all have to be carefully reassembled and the helicopters thoroughly checked. This would take over 18 hours, and is the longest process on the division's schedule.

The 101st Air Assault infantrymen deployed to Egypt in 1982 to take part in Bright Star 82. Their UH-60A helicopters were also deployed. *(Left)*

Blackhawk helicopters arrive at their forward location.

The new D models would be much easier to load, having only 150 hydraulic connectors to take apart. Kiowa and Cobra helicopters are prepared for flight in less than one hour, needing only to have their blades folded and stabilizers removed. The Apache, which will join the division's attack aviation units in 1985, will have similar characteristics.

As a solution for those units which are to be sealifted, the division is now testing a new method of self deployment which will enable the UH-60 and CH-47 to deploy on their own to Europe or the Middle East. The CH-47D does not have problems in flying the distances required for an Atlantic crossing. It has enough fuel for long 'legs' and can refuel aboard amphibious landing support ships such as the *Iwo Jima* and *Tarawa* which can be pre-positioned along the flight route. For the Black Hawk, new external fuel tanks mounted on special racks are now being tested.

Lightweight TACFIRE artillery computers simplify the artillery fire procedures.

A Cobra gunship fires rockets.

An Apache helicopter launches a Hellfire anti-tank guided missile.

A UH-60A Blackhawk flying a Nap of the Earth (NOE) low level flight.

Top: Blackhawk deploys troops to the field.

Above left: A Blackhawk lifts an m-102 howitzer and its ammunition.

Left: Air assault infantryman in action.

MILITARY AIRLIFT COMMAND

Above: An AH-1 Cobra gunship deployed to Egypt by a C-5A Galaxy.

Top right: The CH-47D can lift six inflatable fuel pallets in a single sortie.

Above right: The Blackhawk is squeezed into the C-141.

Below: The CH-47 Chinook is the most complicated equipment to airlift.

Right: Four hours were needed to prepare this Blackhawk for the airlift.

The U.S. Army's New Light Division

Above: A point defense radar used by the 9th Air Defence elements.

Below left: The FAV/TOW combination replaces the M-151A2 TOW Jeep used in other units.

Below: Light earth moving works are carried out by this Honimog mounted system.

Above: The UH-60A armed with scatterable mines in four pods assist the engineer battalion in mining operations.

Left: Dragon missile fired.

In 1981, Gen. E. C. Meyer charged the 9th Infantry Division with 'developing revolutionary approaches in tactics and equipment that can evolve into a new kind of division.' Objectives of such new divisions were to combine the tactical mobility, firepower and survivability of a heavy division with the airlift sustainability required of a light division that could execute worldwide contingency missions while retaining significant utility on the European battlefield, as required by the rapid deployment concepts of both CENTCOM and NATO.

In response to these directives, the US Army selected a team of brilliant 'thinking' officers, many of them with records of innovative, untraditional thinking and independent ideas which they had previously not hesitated to raise. Organized at Fort Lewis, Washington, under the 'High Technology Test Bed' (HTTB) title, they were utilized as a 'think tank' for new and bold ideas which were carried out with the goal of transforming the 9th Infantry into a prototype of the new formation High Technology Light Division (HTLD) not later than 1985.

In January 1983, the COS established ADEA (Army Development and Employment Agency) which, in place of HTTB, is now providing more responsibilities and authority in procuring the testing of high technology toward improving the light infantry divisions.

One of the primary goals of the HTTB, and later ADEA, was to restructure the conventional infantry division unit into a more powerful yet light and mobile force, while reducing the airlift capacity needed for its deployment. Especially adapted for the airland battle doctrine, the new structure required heavy firepower, long range mobility, interdiction capabilities to the enemy's rear elements ('extended battlefield' concept) with light forces and long range weapons, and improved c^3 and real-time information analysis essential for effective targeting and weapons utilization ('integrated battlefield' concepts). In contrast to previous doctrines, the new light division was to use its high mobility instead of armor protection for its survival. Resulting from this concept is the fact that such a division is primarily offensive in nature, as its elements cannot hold ground.

According to current Airland battle doctrine, a high technology light division is to utilize terrain and mobility to expand the fight to the limits of its area of influence using long-range weapons such as TOW and artillery, highly mobile long-range patrols and MLRS, a mission requiring highly integrated and effective command and control facilities. Using small, mobile forces, such elements can contain large enemy formations in an aggressive defense delay action, assisted by improved engineering equipment creating obstacles or, used offensively on the enemy's

flanks and rear, disrupting its lines of communications and hitting high value targets. Such tactics will assist the decisive actions of combined armored forces at the front. Other elements could be used for rear area security and deception, tactics now integrated in the doctrinal concepts.

The HTLD is developed around the flexible skeleton of a self-contained unit, with basic sub-units existing according to the same concepts.

Weight and the number of sorties are the most important factors in deciding which items to take and which to leave. Currently, the HTLD consists of about 14,500 personnel (compared to about 19,000 in a conventional ID). Although a target of 10,000 men was settled upon, a '14K' limit is now thought to be adequate (another evaluation for a '10K extra-light' division is now being looked at in the 7th Infantry).

The three ground brigades consist of a mix of heavy and light combined arms battalions, light attack battalions and strong combat service support elements. Brigade and support elements are also under the division's command. The ground brigades, although having a fixed structure, are task oriented, with combined arms mixing.

HTLD BUILDING BRICKS:
Heavy Combined Arms Battalion (CAB/H)

The division's basic element is the heavy Combined Arms Battalion (CAB/H), of which five are available. (Similar to it, but with a different mix of elements, is the CAB/L, its light brother.) This battalion has a light motorized infantry (LMI) company with all its fighting men grouped in squad carriers, new High Mobility Multiple Wheeled Vehicles (HMMWV) which allow fast cross-country movement and flexibility as a highly mobile weapons platform, ambulance and utility vehicle. The HMMWV will replace the $\frac{1}{2}$t Mule, $1\frac{1}{4}$t Gamma Goat and M151 Jeep. Today, M883 pick-ups are used as surrogate squad carriers, but all 432 HMMWV orders for the division are now scheduled to be received in 1984, completing CAB transition to the new, high mobility vehicles. CAB firepower will consist of squad and personal weapons for medium range, medium- and long-range support with 81 M19 grenade launchers and an anti-tank squad. A heavier assault gun (AG) company will consist of light armored vehicles, of which none are presently available, after the LAV 25 studied for the task was cancelled. The assault gun company fields 12 assault gun vehicles in three platoons and provides heavier and longer-range fire capabilities replacing the MICV in conventional units. The Combat Support Company (CSC) also supports the battalion with Hellfire ground-launch vehicles, heavy mortar platoon (six tubes) towed by HMMWVs, and scouts in high mobility Fast Assault Vehicles (FAV). The light Combined Arms Battalion contains the same units as the CAB/H but in a different

mix – instead of two AG companies, it has only one, with the other replaced by an additional LMI.

Light Attack Battalion

The light attack battalion is the division's most innovative organization, using the speed and maneuverability of its forces to overcome previous limitations. Relying on the new Fast Attack Vehicle (FAV) as its main weapons carrier, this battalion can be moved over all terrain at speeds exceeding 50 mph, replacing the traditional cavalry functions of raiding, recce, etc. With 60 FAVs in the battalion, this unit has only 426 soldiers, of which 186 are actually fighters. It makes the LAB the smallest, most maneuverable fighting ground unit in the division.

The FAV is a unique weapons system. Carrying a TOW or M19 grenade launcher as a standard weapon, this modified 'dune buggie' can travel at speeds of up to 60 mph on rocky surfaces, sand or mud, over obstacles up to two feet high and across others more than a wheel's gap in width, along incredibly steep grades, and 'jump' down from obstacles over ten feet high without losing its speed! Though very effective, the FAV's intensive driving can quickly tire its crew. Thus the units impose a 'drive/rest' program, similar to that used in helicopter units. The M19-equipped FAV also has an M60 MG mounted on the front. This vehicle is excellent for deep-penetration raids, 'silent' long-range patrols, and armor formation engagements at unexpected positions using hard terrain mobility and maximum TOW range (3700 yards). The M19 weapon is effective at distances of up to 2200 yards and can fire AP grenades at high density and with considerable effect. New ammunition is now being developed for limited anti-APC uses. During the HTLD's first full-scale exercise in Summer, 1983, an LAB was pitted against a tank battalion, and the results were astonishing. At a ratio of 3:1 against them, the TOW-carrying FAVs completely defeated the tanks. 'They didn't know where to look or what actually killed them,' said an officer who took part in the 'celebra-

101st Aviation battalion Cobras engage enemy forces from their hidden positions.

An OH-58D AHIP. This helicopter wil greatly enhance the division's recce capabilities.

The Hummer HUMWV, a high mobility vehicle which is being used by most of the division's units, seen here as a troop carrier with M-19 grenade launcher installed.

tion'. With such results, FAVs are seen as the 'aces' of the division's future forces.

Air Attack Cavalry Brigade (CBAA)

This brigade, holding the division's consolidated air assets, has two attack helicopter battalions with 21 Cobras each. Each battalion has three companies with helicopters and crews, and one company of maintenance personnel and facilities. This structure was preferred over the regular combined-elements squadron. The brigade also includes a cavalry squadron of two ground and two air cavalry troops to be armed with new, modified OH-58 Light Air Cavalry Troop (LACT) helicopters, replacing the scout and attack functions of separate helicopters. The LACT will be able to consolidate the two uses on one OH-58 airframe which will carry TOWs or four Stinger AAMs (air/air missiles), air-ground rockets or guns. Each configuration is ready to fly within ten minutes. With AA missiles it will be used against helicopter-hunting HINDs in the forward battlefield. The LACT will not replace the AHIP (Army Helicopter Improvement Program) Aeroscout, which will be used primarily for recce and target marking for long-range guided weapons. In addition, the CBAA has an aviation combat support battalion including two companies of 15 UH-60A Black Hawks each. The UH-60s will be used for creating obstacles with the 'Vulcano' air-scattered mine system, and for forward deployment of light guns, MEDEVAC units, etc., as well as in the assault role.

Divisional Artillery (DIVARTY)

The divisional artillery regiment is based on medium-range weapons. Its main firepower consists of 54 new M198 155mm towed howitzers and nine MLRS. These rocket elements consisting of conventional MLRS cannot be deployed in the C-130 as can other elements in the division. Future types, probably six-rocket packs mounted on M548 tracked vehicles, will be developed, with full air mobility or CH-47 deployment capability.

The guns are organized in three six-gun batteries (18 barrels per battalion). Two additional batteries of six M102 105mm light guns are included in the regiment. The DIVARTY is augmented by advanced target acquisition equipment, such as the APO 36/7 radar, artillery and mortar locators, meteorological survey elements and new lightweight TACFIRE and BCS, and is fully integrated into the command and control network of the division.

THE BOTTOM LINE

In late 1985, the 9th Infantry Division will have been fully converted from a conventional infantry unit into a High Technology Light Division. At the conclusion of testing, the forces will be declared operational. But what will the difference be?

The main advantage of the HTLD will be its rapid deployment capability. Capitalizing on light, lethal weapons systems, small forces can be quickly moved and reach the battlefield with more firepower than regular infantry. In fact, compared to an infantry division, which would require 1480 C-5 and C-141 sorties, the HTLD and its present-generation equipment would be entirely air transportable in only 1349 sorties, switching the C-130 for the huge C-5, while future generation equipment (ITV, heavy trucks, shelters, etc.) will reduce this number even further. The most important factor here is the elimination of C-5-dependent items; the Galaxy is in short supply and dependency on it could limit the division's deployment.

Air-assault (1111 sorties) or airborne divisions (1004) may be more easily deployable by air, but do not have that much firepower and may take a while until established for battle. While the High Technology Light Division cannot replace these airborne or air-assault divisions, it can convert slow infantry into a modern, mobile strike force that can influence the battle much more effectively and with increased survivability. The combination of infantry and high technology can prove much less expensive and more effective than mechanization.

U.S. Marine Aviation

Aviation has played a vital role in the Marine Corps for the past 70 years. While the past accomplishments of the Corps' air arm are both commendable and remarkable, resting upon past laurels has never been a Marine trademark. Marine aviation is no exception. There are four main areas of concern: inventory shortages, aged helicopters, lack of survivable and maintainable airframes, and the requirements for heavier lift capability, as well as more capable assault.

The Corps has come up with a two-prong solution. First, it is participating in a joint service venture to produce an advanced vertical lift aircraft, designated the JVX, by the early 1990s. Secondly, the Corps will buy helicopters now on the market to fill the gap until the other helicopters become available.

The AV-8B Harrier is scheduled to replace the AV-8A version and the A-4M Skyhawk. The B-version has some major improvements over the A-model, including primary payload, flying characteristics in the V/STOL flight regime, weapons delivery systems, and reliability and maintainability. When the Marine Corps receives its full complement of AV-8Bs, it will have 160 in active service which will be placed in eight squadrons.

The F/A-18 program began in July 1982 when El Toro-based Marine Fighter Attack Squadron 314 went to NAS Lemoore, Calif., for six months of F/A-18 transition training. When the squadron returned to MCAS El Toro, California, in January 1983, it received its full complement of 12 F/A-18s.

The Marine Corps' need for heavy lift capability from a helicopter received a 'shot in the arm' when the CH-53E Sea Stallion was introduced to the Corps. The first CH-53E squadron is operating at MCAS(H) New River, North Carolina, with a full complement of 15 aircraft.

Another aircraft the Marine Corps has been looking at is the AH-1T Cobra. Current Marine Cobras will soon be able to fire the Sidewinder missile as well as improved anti-tank weapons, giving them a new air-to-air capability and an increased anti-tank capability.

The two Precision Guided Munitions (PGM) the Corps is looking at are the Hellfire and Laser Maverick. They can take on a threat and beat it without unnecessarily exposing helicopter and fixed-wing aircraft to ground fire.

The fixed-wing side of Marine aviation has not been left defenseless. In the plans for fixed-wing aircraft is the Laser Maverick. The Laser Maverick has a 300-pound warhead, the largest of any US anti-tank PGM. This gives it tremendous deadly strength.

Air Force Units

A 366th TFW F-111 dropping bombs over a desert range.

Although it is the soldiers on the ground who win the wars, it is air power that is most likely to be deployed first in an emergency. Save for Marines, situated close to possible contingency areas, it is USAF AWACS and fighter aircraft which are capable of really rapid deployment. In 1979, a detachment of F-15 Eagles was sent to Saudi Arabia following requests for a 'friendship visit' to deter Iran from possible hostile acts. This was followed by the deployment of four E-3A Sentry AWACS aircraft in 1980, which are now permanently stationed there. Other AWACSes were deployed to Egypt during growing tension on its western border with Chad, and more recently to southern Egypt and Sudan during Libyan operations in Chad and attacks against Sudan. Sophisticated aircraft were now replacing the battleship as a show of force, underlining with their presence US commitments to the safety of the host country with aims toward stabilizing conflicts before their escalation. To meet the requirements of rapid deployment, the USAF allocated several units which are now assigned to CENTCOM under its Central Command Air Force (CCAF) headquarters, made up of a team from the 9th Air Force.

F-15 equipped with FAST packs conformal tanks.

RDF combat aircraft and some of their units

EAGLES

The Langley AFB-based 1st TFW is the USAF's most experienced F-15 squadron. It was the first operational Eagle wing, receiving its first aircraft in January, 1976, becoming fully equipped with 72 aircraft 12 months later. It includes three fighter squadrons and a special maintenance squadron, with separate teams called Aircraft Maintenance Units (AMU), attached to and functioning as part of the operational flying squadrons. Personnel are pre-selected for deployment and are experienced as a team, which includes a crew chief and avionics, munitions and systems specialists. The AMUS follow the F-15s with KC-10s carrying spares and fuel to support the Eagles on the ground during the initial deployment phase. This rather complicated method was adapted in order to cope with the rapid deployment and efficiency standards of the F-15.

During a normal day's flying operations, the wing launches some 66 F-15s on training missions in air/air combat, gunnery, air defense intercepts and air refuelling. On deployments such as the 1979 test move to Saudi Arabia, 12 Eagles flew a total of 122 sorties in 10 days totalling 479.8 hours; the aircraft flew at full mission-capable standards 90% of the time with no major maintenance problems. Other exercises included 'Eagle Thrust' in 1980, in which 66 F-15s demonstrated full mission capability for rapid deployment to Korea. Operated from their home base and two additional sites, the 1st TFW maintained a mission capable rate of 70%; in only eight days the wing flew 813 sorties totalling 975 hours.

It must be kept in mind that the 1st TFW, in its present 'triple-hatted' role, is assigned missions for CENTCOM, Europe and the Far East. To train for these deployments, the wing sends pilots to the 'Maple Flag' exercise at Cold Lake, Canada, to check out, along with other NATO pilots, in a realistic, central-European-like, high threat combat environment, and to 'Red Flag' at Nellis AFB in Nevada for realistic training in desert conditions, also aimed at the general high-threat environment.

The F-15 Eagle is the USAF's primary interceptor and air superiority fighter. With an excellent combination of aerodynamic design, powerplant, firepower and avionics, this fighter is presently unequalled by any of its rivals. Its maximum speed is Mach 2.5 and its flight ceiling is approximately 80,000ft. The Eagle is armed with eight missiles and an internal gun and has an intercept range of over 200 miles, of which some 50 are covered by its internal radar. Although the F-15 can become airborne within six seconds on only 900ft of its Langley runway, it is not likely that the expensive Eagle will be deployed from such surfaces in Saudi Arabia; unfamiliar conditions, a lack of safety features, and the danger of sand, dust and heat can all gang up on the pilot in such demanding operations and put his life, and many millions of dollars worth of aircraft, in great danger.

THUNDERBOLTS

While the F-15s can safeguard the airspace needed for deployment, another type of aircraft might be called in for the dirty work – ground attack. This aircraft is the A-10 Thunderbolt II tank buster. The Thunderbolt II is a specialized aircraft, built to counter the Soviets' numerical tank superiority in a European conflict. The A-10 was designed to fly low and attack tanks quickly from a relatively safe range while withstanding hits from ground fire. It is highly maneuverable, easy to maintain and can fly from secondary airfields at all altitudes in sustained operations in hot or cold weather. Its 30mm Gatling gun can hit and destroy tanks

A-10A Thunderbolt II enters an attack path with a typical sharp turn. Note 'smart bombs' carried: Paveway laser guided, *(right)* and Hobos EO *(left)*.

from beyond 1000 yards, which gives it enough range to egress after a burst without having to overfly the targets themselves. While its capability in a highly sophisticated, dense air defense environment of a possible central European conflict is questioned by several experts, its capability in a low intensity Middle East conflict is unquestionable. Indeed, Thunderbolts were deployed to all the latest Bright Star exercises in Egypt, as well as to Gallant Eagle and others, proving the aircraft's effectiveness in ground support.

The 354th TFW is also a 'triple hat' unit, and training in the wing is both hard and continuous. The unit takes part in many US Army exercises, providing realistic air support, besides flying regular training missions to keep in shape as top marksmen. A-10 pilots of the 354th also participate in 'Red Flag' and 'Maple Flag' exercises and maintain a high rate of overseas deployment to familiarize themselves with both the US Army and its potential 'customers'. A selection of these sorties can be quite impressive: in 1980, elements from the wing's 353rd Squadron deployed to Ft. Irwin, California, for exercise Gallant Eagle 80; to Alberta, Canada, for Maple Flag; to Leck Air Base in Germany for Coronet Mach; and to Alaska for the Brim Frost cold weather exercise. Thunderbolt pilots from the 354th also trained with other RDF units. In 1981, for example, A-10s and the 24th Infantry Division were pitted against a simulated enemy in Exercise Quick Thrust followed by Exercise Crested Cap, part of the annual Reforger training regimen in Europe.

The A-10 is a highly efficient weapon system. A high operational rate and quick turnaround time are the key to this aircraft's combat effectiveness. Regularly operated from inactive, and therefore unprepared, forward locations, A-10 crews have only themselves and the ground support equipment they bring to rely on. The aircraft's designers considered these problems and laid out the Thunderbolt II for easy accessibility and maintenance, and included features such as

A-10A firing its Avenger gun.

A-10A Thunderbolt II is a dedicated
ground support aircraft and represents a
unique concept in US aviation.

F-111s being armed before a training mission.

Facing page: Hill-based 388th TFW Falcon F-16A carrying various weapons and fuel tanks. (Sidewinders on wingtips, bombs under wings and EW pod under the fuselage.)

A-10A firing its 30mm cannon.

built-in test equipment and ladders. Rearming and refuelling are faster due to special equipment developed for the A-10. There is a fast electric ammunition loader for the 30mm cannon, and special fuel bladders for the 'hot refuelling' of the A-10s with their engines on, both shortening turn-around time. A striking example of the A-10's Rapid Arm and Refuel Team's (RAT) effectiveness can be seen during the 354th's annual exercises when over 1000 sorties are flown in 10 days from several for-

ward fields. In rapid deployment exercises, RATS can find themselves in the middle of nowhere, such as the time they stepped out of their C-130 Hercules in the 114 degree heat of a flat, dry lakebed some 15 miles north of Nellis AFB in Nevada. Nevertheless, the RATS maintained a continuous flow of A-10s coming in to refuel and rearm from stocks and supplies carried in the C-130.

In the air, the Warthogs, as the A-10s are called by their pilots, usually operate alongside attack and scout helicopters in the Joint Air Attack Team (JAAT) System. Scouts such as the OH-58 Kiowa spot the enemy and may act as decoys; AH-1 Cobra (or AH-64 Apache) gunships, sometimes along with ground fire, engage anti-aircraft threats in the area with long range ATGWs. Finally, the A-10 tank-busters move in for the kill. The whole team is coordinated by Forward Air Controllers (FACs) in Bronco aircraft, or from the ground. Multiple JAATs are also controlled from EC-130 flying command posts which can also provide Electronic Warfare tactics such as radar or communications jamming in the area of operation.

ONE-ELEVENS

No other USAF aircraft can equal the F-111 for its penetration capability and strike accuracy; its only rival is the European Tornado which is a generation ahead.

Although the One-Eleven, as it is called, is a relatively old design, it is the only USAF aircraft offering all-weather strike capability. The F-111A was flown in combat in Vietnam, operating on low level night missions from Thailand. The aircraft were pitted not only against the worst weather conditions one could think of, but also against sharp terrain contours and enemy SAMs, and the experience became a' lesson well learned by the USAF. (One-Elevens of the 474th TFW flew over 4000 sorties in Southeast Asia with only six losses!) The North Vietnamese feared the F-111 night marauders more than most other US attackers because of the surprise with which they came – at night, without warning, and with large payloads. Today's F-111As look the same as those that fought in Vietnam, but with many modifications introduced according to the bitter lessons of the war.

A more advanced model, the F-

F-111 armed with Mk-82 5001b bombs.

111D, is operated by the 27th TFW. The D-model has improved terrain-following radar, navigation systems and warning devices, and three new computers. It also has a better aerodynamic design, with modified intakes and new engines. Compared to the A-model, the D also has improved air/air capabilities and more accurate air/ground radar performance.

The greatest payoff in F-111 deployment has been its multirole capability in long-range strike missions. Although the performance of this aircraft is most suitable to the terrain and weather of European or Korean conflicts, in Southwest Asia the F-111s can be deployed in a multitude of strikes, some of them tested in Bright Star 83. The aircraft can perform long range attack and interdiction missions well behind enemy lines where opposing forces are less defended and attacks are usually unexpected. F-111s can also undertake anti-ship and sea surveillance missions. A unique F-111 capability is the flying of long range outings involving air-refuelling and the carrying of internal or external weapons loads. Although the F-111 will most probably be used on strike/interdiction operations, aircrews are also training in close air support and air/air profiles. Most F-111 missions are flown below the 200ft level, an altitude relatively safe from detection by enemy radar.

FALCONS

A wing of F-16 Fighting Falcons offers CENTCOM the capability for a wide variety of missions especially suited for the fine weather and conditions prevailing in Southwest Asia.

The F-16A that 388th TFW pilots are flying is one of today's finest aircraft, combining the best abilities of fighters with the top qualities of dedicated attack vehicles. The 388th TFW at Hill AFB, Utah, was the first operational F-16 wing in the USAF, receiving the first aircraft in 1979. Since then, the wing's 16th TFTS (Tactical Fighter Training Squadron) has served to teach other USAF F-16 drivers, as well as foreign Falcon pilots. The rest of the wing's units have participated in numerous exercises and training missions, including hot and cold weather deployments to Europe, Alaska, the Far East and the Middle East. Eight F-16Bs deployed to Egypt for Bright Star 82 and played a key role in the training of new Egyptian pilots selected to fly Egypt's 40 F-16s. Four of the eight two-seat Falcons remained in Egypt for local pilot training, while adding to the USAF instructors' and maintenance crews' experience with desert operations.

F-16A from Nellis AFB deployed to the Carribean on a rapid deployment exercise.

The B-52H used by the SPF can carry bombs on external racks as well as in its weapons bay.

A-7D Corsair aircraft deployed to Egypt on Bright Star 80. They belong to an Air National Guard unit which contributes to the RDF.

The B-52's offensive avionics were upgraded and tested on this aircraft, seen during tests in Edwards AFB, Ca.

Air National Guard A-7D Corsair II from 23rd ANG delivers Mk-82 bombs.

Maverick missiles fired at a tank and effect *(right)*.

STRATOFORTRESSES

An even more impressive, though less flexible force are Strategic Air Command (SAC) B-52 bombers, some which have been converted for conventional bombing with the Strategic Projection Force (SPF). Since its development, the B-52, in its strategic nuclear role, has provided the USAF with an impressive long range attack ability. However, nuclear capability does not deter every enemy, specifically those against which a nuclear strike would not be very practical.

The bombers themselves are old now and can no longer be assured of safely penetrating Soviet airspace. Their replacements, some 100 new B-1B bombers, will enter service only in a few years, at which time the B-52s will be phased out. SAC can now offer to extend the service time of several bomber formations in support of conventional quick-reaction attack anywhere in the world as a feasible solution for initial phase rapid deployment support.

The backbone of the SPF is the B-52H, previously used in the strategic role. The same advantages that served the H-model in its primary strategic mission also serve it in its new tactical mission. The B-52H is capable of flying far greater ranges unrefueled than any other bomber, including the B-52D. While its sophisticated penetration capabilities are not as effective as those of the F-111, the B-52H can use its range advantage in operating from sanctuaries far from the battlefield, thus not having to compete for the limited air bases available in areas closer to the fighting. This also contributes to the giant bomber's survivability. Range advantages also make them independent of air-refueling tankers which are in high demand for other aircraft. Further improving their conventional attack capabilities, the aircraft will soon be equipped with external wing pylons, adding 24 bombs to the 27 500/750lb bomb load carried internally. Accuracy will be improved with a new laser range-finder.

The SPF is assigned two bombardment squadrons and additional com-

An RC-135 ELINT aircraft, part of the
Strategic Projection Force.

mand and intelligence elements from the 57th Air Division, Minot AFB, North Dakota. The principle of SPF operations is the ability to support remotely deployed forces while under direct control of area commanders. To make such a mission feasible, the SPF is structured with all the command and control systems necessary.

The exercise and testing of the SPF has been continuous since 1980. Its first deployment to the Middle East was during Bright Star 82, when bombers flew a 14-hour flight non-stop from Minot to Egypt, dropped a load of bombs at low level prior to a paradrop in a nearby DZ, and returned home. The year after, a detachment of three B-52Hs flew to Egypt for Bright Star 83, operated from Cairo West and tested, together with its command elements, deployment at a forward base. SPF elements also support various exercises around the world, and were recently assigned specific maritime surveillance and anti-ship roles.

The SPF is also responsible on the CENTCOM related reconnaissance aircraft such as the SR-71 Blackbird and TR-1.

EW AIRCRAFT

Other wings and squadrons and their detachments are available to operate under CENTCOM. Among these are the various specialized mission elements such as the 552nd Airborne Warning and Control Wing, flying out of Tinker AFB, Oklahoma, providing command and control facilities with EC-135, EC-130, and E-3A AWACS aircraft.

This is the USAF's most 'combat experienced' wing today, as its aircraft have been sent on numerous missions to deter possible hostile attacks in Southwest Asia, Iceland, the Far East and Europe. Though not actually fighting in a war, their monitoring of enemy aircraft can help prevent one and signifies a US presence.

An F-16A seen at Hill AFB.

Airlift Operations

Because the US Central Command's forces are half a world away from their planned area of operations, getting them to Southwest Asia and then into the battle area itself could be a problem even more serious than the actual fighting. Two basic modes of transportation – airlift and sealift – would be needed. Airlift is fast; an air carrier can bring forces to an airfield close to the battle and return immediately to CONUS, such an operation taking less than 48 hours. Sealift, on the other hand, takes much longer; ships have to be prepared and loaded even before taking into consideration the sea voyage of up to three weeks. Then there is the unloading, a tedious process made even slower by undeveloped ports. The only thing that makes sealift more attractive than airlift is that it can take on extremely heavy and bulky cargo too big even for the USAF's giant C-5 Galaxies.

MILITARY AIRLIFT COMMAND

The Military Airlift Command (MAC) was organized in 1948, consolidating the long-range airlift capabilities of the Air Force and Navy into one non-combatant transport organization then called the Military Air Transport Service (MATS). However, during the widely scattered and remote 'brush fire' wars of the '50s and '60s, the need arose for a quick reacting, highly mobile force able to deter, contain or terminate conflicts. The advent of modern jet airlifters gave MATS the ability to respond to the

80225

MILITARY AIRLIFT COMMAND

c-5A and a c-141A, clearly showing who is the boss here...

Left: The c-141A being 'stretched' at Lockheed assembly lines to become a modernized B model.

c-7 Carribou are among MAC reserve forces, and took part in actions during the Vietnam war.

Above: McDonnell Douglas C-17 will be able to deploy heavy armor units directly to the battlefield area.

Left: Some of the USAF KC-135s were recently reengined with CFM-56 engines.

Far left: Troop transport is facilitated by the use of many airliners under the CRAF program.

Left: The C-130 Hercules is the only type capable of LAPES delivery.

challenge of global airlift and, in 1965, it became the Military Airlift Command. In 1976, MAC became a Specified Command, with better crisis management and airlift resources and a simplified chain of command, coming under the direct control of national authorities.

Central to any analysis of both airlift and sealift capabilities to cope with the needs of rapid deployment is the job each carrier is called upon to do. Airlift is the only transportation mode that can move forces to the trouble area within hours. This speed provides the means to establish an initial defensive position for holding back a threat rather than having to mount a vastly larger force later on to regain lost ground.

The Military Command might be regarded as the adrenalin in the US armed forces bloodstream. It is called upon daily to support forces in fast aerial supply, troop transport, paradrops and training. At war, MAC will perform in two categories: strategic and tactical airlift.

Acting as the fastest means of transporting combat units and equipment to the battle area, primarily from CONUS bases, MAC will be called on to carry out strategic airlift missions world-wide, though its main targets are Europe, the Far East and Southwest Asia. These intercontinental missions are called Intertheater Airlift. Training maneuvers are undertaken annually with Reforger exercises, when elements of CONUS-based divisions designated for European service are transported across the Atlantic. An example of a real strategic airlift operation was the aerial resupply of Israel during the 1973 war, when 566 missions were flown by C-141s and C-5As airlifting some 22,000 tons of supplies from the US.

Tactical airlift, contrary to popular belief, does not consist solely of paradrops; what's more, MAC is not aiming for massive paradrop capability despite the fact that its present force can deploy a full airborne brigade in one drop. More forces could be then airlanded by aircraft touching down at captured airbases. Brigade paradrop capabilities have

never been fully exercised due to budget and operational reasons, and probably never will. However, most of MAC's tactical airlift missions will involve intratheater transport flights, mainly by C-130 Hercules aircraft, with both the air-landing and resupplying of forces already aground in addition to the transporting of troops from strategic airlift bases to the front. In this role, MAC is called on to airlift fighting forces and weapons to the heart of the battle area as it did in Grenada in 1983.

A new role in worldwide MAC duties is the support of special operations, with the infiltration, support and exfiltration of Special Forces units. This role is linked to MAC's rescue units, whose duty is to provide for the recovery of downed airmen during war and emergency rescue missions during peacetime.

THE AIRCRAFT

At present, MAC relies on three basic types of aircraft to accomplish its goals: the C-5A Galaxy, the C-141B Starlifter, and several types of the C-130 Hercules.

In peacetime, MAC operates only with its active forces, while in times of emergency, more wings would be activated. A serious emergency would see the activation of the Civil Reserve Air Fleet (CRAF) program where MAC would take over the oper-

ation of selected civil aviation airliners and freighters to support its operations. CRAF would augment MAC airlift forces, as the badly needed military aircraft would be mostly used for the transport of heavier weapons, vehicles and supplies. In Grenada, for example, MAC operations had to be rescheduled, and some CRAF aircraft were contracted to carry out routine MAC flights while military aircraft flew to the Caribbean. CRAF is not only activated in emergencies; during large exercises, for example, some CRAF aircraft are contracted to test the system and train pilots.

The USAF recognizes three categories of cargo for most military airlift needs. Bulk cargo, such as all types of small items, spares, personal equipment etc., is flown by MAC's smaller cargo transports as well as by CRAF aircraft such as the Boeing 707 and Douglas DC-8. Oversize cargo, such as compact weapons systems, small vehicles and large spares, are transported by larger MAC airlifters such as the C-130 and C-141, or in CRAF wide-body aircraft like the Boeing 747 and McDonnell Douglas DC-10. Modern small to mid-size helicopters were designed to fit into the limited space of these aircraft; AH-64 Apaches and UH-60A Black Hawks, with a bit of squeezing, can be carried in the C-141. The most problematic airlift

MILITARY AIRLIFT OF ONE DIVISION

	INFANTRY*	HTMD	AIR-ASSAULT	AIRBORNE	LIGHT**
SORTIES FLOWN (C-141)	1443	1362	1111	1004	478
CLOSURE TIME (days)	12.4	11.1	9.5	8.5	4

* 19,202 short tons of cargo   ** 12,837 short tons.

goods are outsize cargo such as tanks, heavy helicopters, SP guns and APCs, which must be flown in the giant C-5 Galaxy.

The Lockheed C-5 Galaxy

The Galaxy was designed in the early '60s, with the growing need for global airlift. Utilizing a new turbofan engine and the growing experience with large widebody airframe designs, the USAF called for an aircraft capable of transporting outsize cargo and payloads of over 100 tons for distances of more than 7500 miles while operating from runways as short as 4300 ft. The first C-5A flew in 1966, but the high hopes the Air Force had for it did not materialize; while the aircraft fulfilled size and weight carrying requirements, actual performance regarding flight range and runway lengths were not satisfactory. Later, inflation reduced the number of aircraft purchased from 115 (six squadrons) to 81 (four squadrons), delivery being in the early '70s. But the Galaxy was, and still is, an excellent outsize cargo airlifter equipped with access doors and ramps fore and aft, allowing the easy loading and unloading of cargo; its low ground clearance and wide body design make it the only airlift solution

for tanks and heavy helicopters such as the Chinook.

Time has been another problem, with C-5A structural fatigue developing somewhat earlier than expected. A new wing for the aircraft was proposed by Lockheed, and modifications are now being carried out on the remaining 77 C-5As in service, with the retrofitting to be completed by 1987. An improved model, the C-5N, was the successful Lockheed proposal for the C-X competition, chosen basically due to funding practicalities. Fifty of the aircraft were ordered in 1982 and officially designated the C-5B. This aircraft will incorporate all retrofit modifications made for the C-5A, with new TF39-1C engines, restructured wings, and improved maintainability, which proved rather costly on the A-models.

The Lockheed C-141 Starlifter

In the late '50s, MATS anticipated an airlift shortfall, as the C-133 Cargomaster it had at the time could not fulfill the growing need for air transport. A new swept wing Lockheed design with a full section ramp/door, side paradrop exits, power reversers and all-weather capabilities, the C-141A was one of the world's most

advanced airlifters at the time. However, there were some features lacking in the design. Cargo was limited to the basic requirements of the late '50s and, without air refuelling, range was a severe limitation.

These problems were recently overcome with the modification of the 274 A-models remaining in service. The basic A-model could take 154 troops, 123 paratroopers or 80 stretchers in a MEDEVAC role, with a total payload capability of 5290ft³. The modified B-model has an increased payload capability of 30% made possible by an additional fuselage section almost $23\frac{1}{2}$ feet long between the flight deck area and the wing's leading edge. In addition, an air refuelling receptacle and new fuel system plumbing have given the new Starlifter unlimited range.

The Lockheed c-130 Hercules

The Hercules is the tactical airlift workhorse in MAC service. Another Lockheed design, the c-130 was developed to answer the needs identified during operations in the Berlin airlift and Korean campaign. The Hercules' high wing provides an unobstructed cargo compartment; its flat, level floor enables easy loading and unloading; and its flight

Above: An xm-765 loaded on to a yc-14.

Above left: the yc-14 was the only aircraft capable of airlifting tanks to forward airfields.

Left: yc-14 could use short runways using its special wing design which adds lift on takeoff and landing.

McDonnell Douglas yc-15 four engined STOL transport seen during its flight tests.

Top left: Air refuelling capability was added to the upgraded Starlifter C-141B.

Left: EC-130 flying command post and EW station.

Above: KC-135A refuels a C-5A Galaxy.

characteristics allow short field capabilities. A more powerful model, the C-130B, first flew in 1958, and a further improved version, the C-130E, took to the air in 1961. C-130H models were received in 1975. Special C-130 models include the extended range HC-130H, the EC-130E flying command post (with EW capability), the WC-130E weather reconnaissance aircraft, the MC-130E special operations aircraft (a new model, the MC-130H, is now being purchased), the AC-130E airborne gunship, and many others.

The McDonnell Douglas KC-10

The KC-10 is a DC-10 widebody commercial aircraft modified for specific military use. The availability of widebody commercial aircraft as a solution to airlift shortfalls did not escape Defense Department attention. However, redesigning aircraft such as the Boeing 747, Lockheed L-1011 or DC-10 for general aircraft use proved uneconomical due to structural problems, wing location, cargo compartment size, fuselage configuration and price. For specific roles, however, DOD decided that modified airliner airframes could be successful.

The Air Force identified the need for a dual purpose tanker/cargo plane for which a modified DC-10 was selected in 1977. The KC-10 can follow air force aircraft deployed abroad, with maintenance personnel, spare parts and supplies in addition to fuel, thus consolidating the roles of the separate KC-135 tanker and C-130 and C-141 cargo aircraft normally used for these purposes. The KC-10 can carry more fuel than its predecessor, can refuel aircraft faster, and take up to 27 standard cargo pallets in addition to its fuel load. A total of 44 KC-10 aircraft will be flying by the end of the decade.

THE CHALLENGE

Since 1974, at least 17 major mobility studies comparing established airlift requirements to available capabilities found serious MAC deficiencies. The latest found a 50% shortfall rate in the present minimum airlift capability of 30.4 million metric tons/day – intratheater airlift needs are estimated at 66 million tons/day.

If the time ever comes, MAC may find itself with ample troop space, but only enough room for a fraction of their 'rolling formations'. Tanks, APCs and supplies would all have to wait for sealift, which is also in short supply. Today's MAC airlift shortfall is both in intertheater and intratheater missions. Further complicating this matter, the Army's new Air-land doctrine will demand even greater intratheater airlift and aerial resupply capabilities. The new doctrine calls for the rapid movement of forces and equipment to forward battle areas, and laterally across the theater as the battle develops. To support this con-

The KC-10A is a modified DC-10 and serves the USAF as both tanker and transport aircraft.

cept, increased levels of both inter- and intratheater airlift will be needed, with outsized cargo, airdrop and airland capability, and with improved STOL performance and survivability.

Growing demands for airlift due to the increasing commitments in CENTCOM's area of operations make intertheater operations even more demanding. As already said, with present fleet space, MAC can transport only 30.4 million metric tons daily, as compared with the present need for 66. To make things even worse, the aircraft presently in MAC inventory are getting older. For intertheater operations, C-141s will most likely be phased out soon after the turn of the century. The C-5A is considered capable of remaining in MAC service at least until the second decade of the next century, as are the C-5B and KC-10. For intratheater airlift, A- and D-model Hercules will be retired beginning at the turn of the century, with the B-, E- and H-models to remain on at least until 2010, aided by wing structure modifications and a modernization program mainly in avionics.

Much funding was invested since 1974 in trying to overcome this airlift shortfall. Plans were formulated, tests were held, and many dollars spent on two projects that could have

solved the problem. The first was a study of two new aircraft to replace the C-130, the McDonnell Douglas YC-15 and Boeing YC-14 STOL jet transporters. If adopted, these aircraft would have solved many of MAC's present problems. For example, the YC-14 prototype enhanced the mobility of M60 tanks, APCs and other outsize cargo, including M109 SP guns and 175mm howitzers, which were then considered non-air transportable. The YC-15 prototype was equipped with the most advanced features then available. Both designs were promising, but costs eventually went too high.

A second study was mounted to select a new intertheater aircraft designed to augment the C-5's capabilities, but utilizing unimproved landing fields. The study, taking several years, settled on a new aircraft to be called C-X, but the House allowed it to die a slow death for financial and bureaucratic reasons.

However, pressure steadily grew until the plan was revived in early 1984, and the C-X was at last designated the C-17. For the original C-X, Boeing had proposed a new three engine design; McDonnell Douglas came up with a four engine aircraft; and Lockheed handed in a design

based on its C-5A. Soon, the competition was narrowed down to the redesigned C-5 and the McDonnell Douglas plan. To these proposals, a modified Boeing 747 and KC-10 were added. While the McDonnell Douglas aircraft eventually was selected, uncertainty remains – the Air Force already decided to purchase more C-5Bs to augment its present and near future force of Galaxies, but has also requested continued funding for the C-17.

The McDonnell Douglas C-17

Until recently referred to as the C-X, the C-17 will be a tremendous addition to MAC inventories and a sorely needed vehicle to augment the presently inadequate airlift capabilities. It will be what the early widebody airliners were to the airlines: everything dreamed of, and much more.

The C-17 is designed to be a 'direct delivery airlifter,' which means that the US will not need a special intratheater airlifter to fly from the rear to the front – the C-17 will be able to transport troops and equipment directly from bases in the US to the battle area.

A great benefit of the C-17 is that it is built for outsize cargo. It will be the only aircraft, apart from the C-5A/B, able to carry every type of combat

equipment used by the Army and the Marines. Unique to the C-17 will be its ability to airdrop or LAPES outsized vehicles, something C-5s are unable to do. The outsize cargo carrying capability will enable heavy weapons such as tanks, artillery pieces and attack helicopters to be committed to combat immediately after off-loading. Two infantry fighting vehicles (IFVs), two 8 x 8 five ton trucks plus trailers side by side, and two jeeps plus trailers might be a typical wartime load. Four UH-60 Black Hawks, ready to fly within an hour after off-loading, could be transported in another scheme. To underline the C-17's intratheater airlift capabilities, it is interesting to compare it with the present MAC aircraft – the C-17, according to McDonnell Douglas, will be able to carry the maximum payload of the C-130H on its aft cargo ramp alone!

For a successful airlift mission, the ability to use available short and narrow unimproved runways and facilities is necessary. In this respect, the C-130 has no rivals; its operational requirements permit it to use runways as short as 3000ft, due to its relatively small dimensions. The huge C-17, however, will need just under twice the area of the C-130's turnaround circle, and the

Above: A C-141B Starlifter.

Left: A C-130 Hercules using LAPES drops cargo at a forward field.

Right: WC-130H weather reconnaissance aircraft.

same area for parking. It will have unique capabilities due to special design features such as winglets enabling shorter wing span, externally blown flaps (derived from the YC-15) allowing safe short runway operations, and supercritical wings reducing drag weight and fuel consumption. It will also be powered by advanced turbofan engines which will be more fuel efficient and require less maintenance time than present power plants. It is assumed that, if financial obstacles are cleared, the first C-17 will enter service in the early 1990s.

A current 'Airlift Master Plan' has evaluated US airlift needs for the next 30 years, and calls for a balanced force consisting of C-5s, C-141s, C-17s and C-130s, plus the available assets of the Air Force Reserve and Air National Guard. The master plan recommended the purchase of 180 new C-17s to best satisfy the needs for both inter- and intratheater airlift and add to MAC's somewhat lacking outsize cargo capability. The introduction of the C-17 will, at last, meet the minimum daily airlift goal of 66 million metric tons and also increase intratheater capability by 78%. It will also, of course, modernize the force and compensate for the retirement of early C-141 and C-130 models.

The order for 50 new C-5B Galaxy aircraft will also provide an airlift capability increase, mainly for outsize cargo. As mentioned before, compared to the C-17, the C-5B is more restricted to large airport facilities and is therefore limited in deployment. It will, however, be able to fill a near term airlift requirement with a proven design. C-5As will be transferred to USAF Reserve units, therefore extending their life cycles by reducing peacetime flight hours.

In regards to the special needs of operations in Southwest Asia, MAC faces a serious deficiency in operational airbases and overflight rights, in addition to its present shortfall in airlift capacity. Considering the C-5A, few bases in the region could support its operations. Egypt's Cairo West air base, the main civilian airports in Saudi Arabia, Israel's Ben Gurion airport and Uvdah air base, and airports in the UAE and Kuwait could be used, but there has been a reluctance by local governments to lend support, even for their own sake, to US forces, as was so clearly demonstrated in Spring 1984 when American proposals to secure the Gulf shipping lanes were turned down. Facilities which have been improved with US funds might be used, such as Oman's Masirah air

base with its 10,200ft runway, and Egypt's Ras Banas airfield, with two parallel fighter-type runways. The Seeb airfield near Muscat has an 11,800ft runway. Only 11,000⁺ft runways with ample turn space can handle the C-5A, and not a single runway in the area can accommodate the B-52H. Somalia has a 13,550ft runway at Berbera that has been made available to the US (although having been built by the Soviets), but the area lacks additional facilities and can be used only for refuelling with fuel specially flown in. An airfield at Mombasa, Kenya, has a 10,650ft runway and improved taxiways, making it feasible for USAF and USN operations.

The need for massive C-130 operations in Middle East contingency intratheater airlift is therefore obvious. Not just austere airfield capability is needed, but also all types of airdrop capabilities, as in most locations there are barely dirt roads, never mind unpaved landing strips. But then there is the problem of the C-130 fleet's oversize cargo restrictions...

C-130s will probably come first from Rhine Main airbase in Germany, which is the nearest Hercules base. However, there are not enough Hercules stationed there to support

even a low scale deployment in Southwest Asia. Further reinforcement from CONUS would therefore be needed to support deployment to the Middle East. As the C-130 does not have aerial refuelling capabilities, Hercules will have to cross the Atlantic by 'island hopping'. This is costly, both in time and money, and a major obstacle to any deployment. Until the aircraft arrive, forces already deployed would have to rely on host nations for air transport which, although regularly carried out in the RDF's Bright Star exercises, would remain, at best, an uncertainty. Thus, the C-17 is looked to for the transport of badly needed supplies such as tanks, APCs, SP guns, radars and command posts directly to the battle area from the continental US, something that could save the day for MAC in a rapid deployment contingency.

U.S. Navy – Naval Forces and Power Projection

The USS Eisenhower nuclear powered carrier.

Traditionally, naval forces represented a nation's power, as sea voyage was once the only means of international travel. In the 20th century, naval power is no less important. Most world trade is dependent upon ships, and narrow sea straits and strategic locks are more important than ever before.

Naval forces of all the superpowers sail the open seas, maintaining their presence in vital spots. In conflict, each fleet would try to prevent its opponent from taking control of the oceans, thus ensuring its own access to vital shipping lanes for both military and commercial reasons. Another naval role is to project force to distant areas. The US Navy maintains a strong force, Task Force 77 (part of the Seventh Fleet), with an aircraft carrier and its escort off Southwest Asia. Another force, usually stationed in the eastern Mediterranean, frequently cruises the Red Sea as well.

The US Navy, the world's largest naval force, is committed to both sea control and force projection missions. It undertakes these roles with its basic fighting units, the Aircraft Carrier Task Force.

THE CARRIER TASK FORCE

The mainstay of the US Navy is its 13 aircraft carriers deployed throughout the world. They are escorted by several additional ships, each charged with defending the carrier from other surface ships, submarines, aircraft and missiles. Other vessels carry supplies for the group.

The aircraft carriers are of two basic types: nuclear powered (CVN) and conventional powered (CV). Nuclear powered carriers are more capable of extended periods on station. They can carry more fuel and spares, never mind more aircraft, in the additional room afforded by the minimum space required for nuclear fuel.

Currently under construction are the Nimitz-class nuclear powered aircraft carriers. The *Nimitz* (CVN-68) was the first of this class, and the second to be deployed by the US Navy (the first being the Enterprise-class,

of which only one ship was constructed). The *Nimitz* was followed by the USS *Eisenhower* (CVN-69) and the USS *Carl Vinson* (CVN-70). Still to come are the *Theodore Roosevelt* (scheduled for 1987), and the *Abraham Lincoln* and *George Washington*, which will bring the US Navy to its target level of a 15-carrier fleet.

The capability to deploy 15 carrier battle groups will enable the Navy to maintain a presence at or near every vital world spot, while also maintaining a presence on the open seas. In order to maintain this number, several of the older, conventional carriers will have to be modernized under a Service Life Extention Program (SLEP). The *Saratoga* was modernized in 1983, followed by the *Forrestal* in 1984.

The peacetime actions of the carrier task forces can be impressive, judging by the 1983 odyssey of the USS *Ranger* battle group. Deploying from its home port in July, the task force set sail to the Pacific but diverted on short notice to waters off the Central American coast. After a short period, the force returned to its assigned area in the western Pacific, but with escalating tension in the Persian Gulf, the *Ranger* was ordered to the Indian Ocean. At the same time, the battle group stood by to deploy to Lebanon. The *Ranger* and its group

Above: EA-6B Prowler, fighting
electronics with electronics.

Above, right: LAMPS III, the new ASW
helicopter based on a SH-60B version.

Top left: The aircraft carrier, mainstay
of the US Navy's task force.

An Intruder equipped with the TRAM
sights.

Left: A-6E Intruder, carrier operated all-
weather attack aircraft.

Below right: A pilot view of a refuelling
from a KA-6C.

Left: The carriers front line of defense,
the F-14 Tomcat.

Below: KA-6C tanker.

A-7E Corsair II, the US Navy principal light attack aircraft.

ships later deployed to the South China Sea and, after 122 days without having put into port, was relieved by the USS *Midway*.

NAVAL AVIATION

US naval aviation is no less impressive than the Navy's surface force. With its carrier-deployable aircraft, the Navy is capable of performing all military missions from its battle groups, short of heavy lift transport.

Facing page, above: The airborne early warning aircraft, E-2C.

Facing page, below: RH-53 mine countermeasures helicopter on manoeuvers with an MCM ship.

Standard ship/air medium range missile. A new version of extended range missile is now in production.

The US Navy/Marines new F/A-18 Hornet attack/fighter.

New Jersey, the first of four battleships returned to active service.

Bottom: Rolling Airframe Missile (RAM), a new concept for short range/point defense ship protection.

GRUMMAN F-14A TOMCAT

The Tomcat is the US Navy's primary interceptor. It is one of the world's most advanced fighters, equipped with a weapons system unmatched by any other of today's aircraft. Operating alongside Hawkeye early warning aircraft, the Tomcat can intercept planes well beyond the enemy's effective range, therefore providing the carrier with an 'outer defense zone'.

The F-14A is powered by two Pratt & Whitney TF-30-412A afterburning turbofans, and can reach speeds of over Mach 2.3. Its primary weapons system consists of up to six ultralong range Pheonix air/air missiles, or shorter-ranged, but lighter Sparrow or Sidewinder missiles. All weapons are controlled by an internal system built around the superb AWG-9 radar/fire control system. Tomcats were successfully deployed in air combat in 1981, shooting down two Libyan SU-22s which penetrated the USS *Nimitz's* outer defense zone in the Gulf of Sidra. In Lebanon, Tomcats were frequently deployed as recce aircraft equipped with TARPS pods, a compact package of aerial cameras and data link communications.

MCDONNELL DOUGLAS F-4 PHANTOM

Until the introduction of the Tomcat, the Phantom was the US Navy's primary fighter. The F-4 is a tough,

An F/A-18 launches a Sidewinder missile.

powerful, multirole fighter used in intercept, fighter and attack roles. On intercept missions, the F-4 can carry eight AAMs, four of them Sparrows and four Sidewinders. Its air/ground weaponry includes guided missiles and bombs, free-fall weapons and rockets. The Phantom saw intense action in Vietnam and is now deployed as a primary fighter aboard some of the older carriers. The Phantom is being replaced by the F/A-18 as the Marines' primary fighter, deployed from carriers or expeditionary airfields to maintain air superiority over the Marine battlefield.

MCDONNELL DOUGLAS F/A-18 HORNET

The Hornet will inject new blood into the aging fleet of US Navy and Marine aircraft. The multirole jet will have a primary attack mission, but will maintain good fighter capability, even with a full bomb load. The Hornet's primary air combat weaponry will be two Sidewinders and two Sparrows (later to be replaced by AMRAAM, which will be controlled by the Hornet's advanced APG-65 radar, the most sophisticated fighter/attack radar ever developed. The F/A-18's ground attack weapons will consist of free fall bombs and rockets, as well as various guided munitions. The first Marine wing flying Hornets has been operational since 1983, while the first Navy squadron will receive its aircraft in 1985.

VOUGHT A-7E CORSAIR II

The Corsair is the mainstay of the present carrier battle group's light attack force. It has medium range, fine weather attack capability. Its excellent navigation and weapons delivery system enable its pilot to mount a precise first-pass attack. However, the Corsair is rather limited in its weapon load and weather condition capability.

GRUMMAN A-6E INTRUDER

The twin-engine Intruder is the task force's night claws. It is the only carrier-deployed aircraft with good all-weather/night attack capability,

AV-8B, the new V/STOL aircraft now entering USMC service.

being equipped with superb radar, night vision devices and sophisticated weapons delivery systems. Utilizing the whole spectrum, from microwave (radar imagery) to visible light (TV guidance), the Intruder's new TRAM (Target Recognition Attack Multisensor) system can spot and track targets and guide sophisticated weapons to the attack.

As adverse weather and night flying require the full concentration of the pilot, the second crewman, the bombardier/navigator, operates all the Intruder's sophisticated systems. A modified version is the KA-6C flying tanker, also operated by the air wing.

This is a key aircraft for deployment on a carrier as it is needed for returning aircraft, too low on fuel to remain airborne until they can be recovered on the carrier's single landing facility. The tanker can also follow strike forces into enemy airspace, providing aircraft with fuel for extended range operations. The D-model is now coming into service. The Intruder is also deployed by the Marines in the same roles.

GRUMMAN EA-6B PROWLER

The Prowler is a modified A-6E, stripped of its conventional weapons and loaded with advanced electronic

161

warfare equipment. The ALQ-99 electronics set provides the Prowler's four-man crew with the capability to locate, identify and disrupt enemy communications, radar and weapons control systems. The crew can activate multiple jammers simultaneously against several targets or concentrate on the massive jamming of a single threat. EA-6Bs are usually deployed at standoff range, engaging the enemy radars from a safe distance and allowing friendly attacking aircraft to approach their targets undetected. The Prowler can also intercept the guidance signals of anti-ship missiles fired by enemy aircraft, preventing them from engaging their targets. The EA-6B is also used by the Marines.

GRUMMAN E-2C HAWKEYE

The Hawkeye was the world's first effective early warning aircraft. Its ability to spot aircraft at over-the-horizon ranges led to the AWACS concept for the USAF. The Hawkeye is itself an unimpressive design, but when performance is considered, the aircraft is unparallelled. Its General Electric TPS-125 radar can spot any target, on the surface or in the air, at ranges of 100 to 250 miles. The Hawkeye's reliable flight systems ensure long on-station time, and its slow landing speed and rugged gear ensure safe carrier deployment. The E-2C's electronics systems enable data transfer from its airborne radar to the carrier's battle information center and, at the same time, to the carrier's interceptors. Its new data links enable its radar operators not only to track every aircraft, but also to fire the F-14's missiles at selected targets, something Tomcat pilots would no doubt protest.

LOCKHEED S-3A VIKING

The Viking is a small, twin-engine anti-submarine aircraft, usually operating in an ASW team with the carrier's SH-3H helicopters. It is equipped with sophisticated on-board sensors and can drop expendable sonar probes and passive listening devices. The Viking can attack submarines with bombs, depth charges, rockets or torpedos.

Above: The YAV-8B Harrier II prototype. Note the variety of weapons carried.

Left: The S-3A Viking ASW aircraft.

Right: The US Navy new MH-53E mine counter measures helicopter.

Left: The Navy's 'electronic fox', EA-6B Prowler.

Below: The battleship New Jersey. Note the 16″ guns at fore and aft.

NORTH AMERICAN RA-5C VIGILANTE

The RA-5C was once the US Navy's most sophisticated aircraft. Initially designed as the supersonic A-5 high-altitude bomber, it was converted to the reconnaissance role due to changes in operational requirements and soaring costs. The Navy packed the Vigilante's weapons bay with cameras and remote sensing and communications equipment, and, since the Vietnam conflict, has deployed the aircraft in the recce role. Aboard F-14-equipped carriers, the Vigilante has been replaced by Tomcats carrying TARPS pods. A specially developed RF-18 may replace both the RA-5C and F-14/TARPS in the reconnaissance role.

AV-8B HARRIER II

The US Marines operate two STOL versions of the Harrier, the AV-8A, produced for the USMC and which follows the basic British Harrier design, and the brand new Harrier II, an advanced version with more powerful engines, higher payload capability and more reliable systems.

The Harrier has the unique ability to take off and land vertically (VTOL), which means that it can be operated from short-decked carriers like the LHA, a large amphibious landing vessel, or be deployed to forward landing strips on highways or expeditionary air bases built in the deployment area by Marine construction teams.

BATTLESHIP BATTLE GROUPS

A relatively old concept has been revived with the reactivation of the first of four Iowa-class battleships, the USS *New Jersey* (BB-62), in 1983. (A second ship, the USS *Iowa* (BB-61), will enter service in 1984 and be followed by two additional battle wagons, the USS *Missouri* and USS *Wisconsin*.

The *New Jersey's* first deployment provided an example of its capabilities. Departing a month earlier than the USS *Ranger* (see beginning of this chapter), the *New Jersey* arrived in the western Pacific for a short shakedown cruise. On its return to its home port it was diverted to a station off the Central American coast in order to maintain a naval presence there during an especially heated period in the local conflict. Then the *New Jersey* was ordered to sail to the eastern Mediterranean to support the US Marine peacekeeping forces in Beirut. While there, the ship saw action for the first time since Vietnam, where she took part in coastal bombardment during 1968-9. Although the battleship's heavy bombardments of Syrian and Moslem/Druse positions near Beirut did not end the conflict, they offered the Marines a few days of quiet.

Heavy and slow-firing guns have been retired, along with their ships, in favor of smaller, lighter missile-capable vessels. But with the return of the battleships, Marines now have badly needed firepower they can rely on for their operations. Eventually, each forward deployed MAU will have a battleship for support.

MINE COUNTERMEASURES CAPABILITY

As part of its role in sea control, the US Navy must prevent vital sea lanes from being blocked by mines or enemy fire. Since the total blocking off of the open seas is impossible, such actions are focused on narrow waterways such as the Malakka Straits, Straits of Hormuz and Bab el Mandeb, as well as heavily travelled sea routes. The blocking of these vital routes would likely be broken by a massive US naval operation, but their mining would be relatively easy and pose a great danger to civilian and military shipping in that area.

In order to counter such a threat, the US Navy has several mine countermeasures ships which can clear a safe passage through sea obstacles. Until recently, the US had been totally dependent on host nation support in the minesweeping of a contingency area, while maintaining only a small fleet of 21 ocean going vessels for carrier battle group defense. This aging fleet will be augmented by 14 new mine countermeasures ships of the MCM-1 type, the first, the *Avenger*, already being built. The new MH-53E mine countermeasures helicopter will add to the MCM-1's capabilities.

U.S. Marines

Above: A USMC CH-46 Sea Knight helicopter landing troops.

Left: A Marine opens fire from his LTVP-7 turret-mounted M-85 gun.

Above right: CH-53 Stallion landing troops.

Below right: Marine M-60A1 tank swims ashore.

Facing page: US Marines landing in Beirut.

Below: LTVP-7s on beach assault.

Among the best American units, and with a substantial combat record to prove it, are the Marines. The Marine Corps was established by the Continental Congress on 10 November 1775. Continental Marines enlisted for duty aboard a particular ship; there were no ground components – only shipboard detachments acting as snipers and boarders during close-in battles.

It was not until 1834 that separate Marine units were formed for service on land. Around 1900, when steamships began outnumbering sailing vessels and coal was needed for fuel, the Marines were required to guard coastal stations. As the Navy could not build a force large enough to sustain refueling locations worldwide, it had to be prepared to seize such bases by force if needed. This task was at first given to a unit composed of sailors and Marines, but later this was reduced to the Marines, who were specially trained and always ready for deployment. The climax of Marine operations was reached in WW II, when the names Guadalcanal, Tarawa and other Pacific islands entered into military history as jewels in the crown of amphibious warfare, with tales of bravery setting the standards for years to come. It was in World War II where the foundations for amphibious warfare were set, and on which the heritage of the present day USMC is built.

The Marines hold a unique role in the US military. As a maritime nation with worldwide commitments, the US needs to maintain control of the open seas to enable force projection for the defense of its interests. These needs are fully supported by the combination of the Navy and the Marines.

Linked from the very beginning, they have become fully dependent upon one another: vessels for transport and amphibious assault, which the Marines don't have, are provided by the Navy, while troops for amphibious landing and coastal deployment, which the Navy doesn't have, are provided by the Marines.

Historically, the Marines were always the First to Fight. With little or no warning, they have often been thrust into action, such as that in Gre-

Above left: LTVP passing the high surf.

Left: TOW jeeps operated by the Marines.

Above: B-300 SMAW operated by the Marines.

Facing page, top left: USMC AH-1T Cobra gunships.

Facing page, left: A USMC M-151A2 TOW Jeep.

Facing page, below: Marines training Camp at Lejeune 'combat town'.

Below: CH-53 taking Marines on a heliborne assault.

nada during October 1983 when the 22nd Marine Amphibious Unit, on its way to Lebanon, was sent without prior notice to land on the Caribbean island and fight there alongside Army Rangers. In recent years, however, the commitment of Marine units to far away contingencies has increased as the US put a higher priority on Southwest Asia. This desert area, with its barely-developed infrastructure, demands more range and capabilities, while its rough coastlines offer few locations for amphibious operations.

Today's Marines have not changed since the Korean War when the Corps' peacetime strength was set at three active divisions plus one in reserve, giving an active manpower level of about 190,000 troops, with another 40,000 if need be. Units are stationed at CONUS bases and at forward positions abroad.

Three Fleet Marine Forces (FMF) provide the Corps with its primary landing capabilities:

I FMF is based in California on the US west coast and can be deployed for South/Central American contingencies, or emergencies in Northeast Asia. Its major elements are the 1st Marine Division, based at Camp Pendleton, its combat service support group, the 3rd Marine Air Wing, based at MCAS El Toro, and the 7th Marine Amphibious Brigade (MAB), based at Twentynine Palms, where it is used as the training cadre at the Marines Air-Ground Combat Center. This MAB has its equipment and supplies prepositioned with the NTPF (Near-Term Prepositioned Force) at Diego Garcia, and is the Marines' primary rapid deployment component for a Southwest Asian contingency.

III FMF operates in the central and western Pacific. It is composed of the 3rd Marine Division, based on Okinawa along with the 1st Marine Air Wing, the III's air support unit. The division's 1st Brigade is stationed in Hawaii. This force also provides an MAU continuously stationed in the Indian Ocean and the Persian Gulf as part of the 7th Fleet.

II FMF, based on the eastern US coast, is the Marines' tactical arm for

Above: The Super Cobra is now proposed by Bell to update the USMC Cobra fleet.

Facing page, above: A USMC TOW Jeep landing from an LCU in Beirut.

Facing page, left: Marines dismounted from an LTVP.

Facing page, right: M-88 armoured recovery vehicle, operated by the Marine's FSSG.

Left: Heliborne assaults replaced many of the amphibious operations.

Atlantic deployment. This force is primarily oriented toward NATO contingencies, with its main objectives being Norway and the Mediterranean. Its major elements are the 2nd Marine Division, stationed at Camp Lejeune, and the 2nd Air Wing, based at Cherry Point MCAS. This force has an MAU routinely deployed in the Mediterranean with the 6th Fleet and occasionally sent to the Red Sea and Indian Ocean.

The current Marine mission is to project sea power ashore, either by amphibious or air-assault means, or both. Amphibious assault calls into play the combined Navy/Marine Corps team with a fully-integrated amphibious assault employing all elements of Navy combat power in support of the Marine air-ground task force in both helicopter and surface landings on a hostile shore.

Even under the most favorable conditions, the amphibious assault is one of the most complex types of military operations, but is also one of the strongest means of conventional power projection against a relatively sophisticated enemy as compared to other means such as paradrop, air attack or off-shore presence.

The Marines provide the US with its only forcible entry option against a well-defended enemy. The Marines can proceed, without interruption, from a naval to a land campaign. They have the inherent capability to build a strong fighting force ashore, utilizing all the necessary elements of a combined-arms combat power.

THE MARINE AIR-GROUND TASK FORCE

The Marine Corps is unique among the US services because it possesses a full range of capabilities, from bayonets to nuclear weapons-carrying aircraft, all tuned for a combined-arms effort in amphibious assault and inland operations. The Marine Air-Ground Task Force (MAGTF) has been set up to conduct combat operations, taking maximum advantage of the combat potential inherent in a closely integrated air-ground team and putting it under the direction and control of a single commander. Marines can be transported by both

Above: The powerful new CH-53E helicopters can take the M-198 gun and its ammunition in one sortie.

Facing page, above: Marine's assault exercise at Garrucha, Spain.

Facing page, below: The AAVs swim ashore.

Right: The Cobra gunship seen on a helicopter carrier deck.

The Marine's Sea Knight CH-46 helicopter.

Marines seen on an LTVP-7 deck.

Marines dismount from their AAV.

174

air- and sealift, but for full power deployment they need both. Therefore, the MAGTF can operate either as a naval entity or as part of a combined task force in addition to its capability for deployment as a separate service component.

The MAGTF is a task-organized force; therefore, flexibility is the key for its successful operation. It generally includes four major components:

a ground combat element, which may range from battalion to division-sized units and includes infantry, tanks, recce, combat engineers, artillery, and amphibious assault vehicles;

an aviation element, including both fixed-wing and rotary-wing aircraft, ranging from the composite squadron level to one or more wings, offering offensive air support and air superiority, assault support, close air support, air reconnaissance, electronic warfare, command and control;

a combat support element ranging in size from a Marine Amphibious Unit service support group to a Force Service Support Group (FSSG), tailored to provide a total range of logistics support to include supply, maintenance, engineering, motor transport, and medical and dental services; and

a command element providing a single headquarters for command and control of the whole task force, including air, ground, amphibious and support forces.

For specific missions against enemy forces, the MAGTF can put together three basic formations.

The Marine Amphibious Unit (MAU)

This is the smallest air-ground task force, normally regarded as a battalion-size unit containing the following forces:

infantry, reinforced by tank, anti-tank, artillery, recce and Amphibious Assault Vehicle (AAV) and combat engineer units to form a Battalion Landing Team (BLT). The strength of this battalion was recently cut by 10%, but its firepower has been increased by 25%;

a composite aircraft squadron con-

The Marines will operate these tilt rotor aircraft which will replace some of their helicopter fleet toward the early 90s.

The heaviest artillery in USMC inventory, the M-107 175mm gun.

175

The SEAD

(SUPPRESSION OF
ENEMY AIR DEFENSE) TEAM

In assault using both air and ground elements, the true spirit of combined-arms operations can be seen. In today's dense and highly sophisticated battlefield, low level air operations such as those carried out by Marine aviators are highly dangerous. Fraction-of-a-second coordination must be kept with ground forces, which are responsible for the suppression of enemy air defenses and the directing of fire in the path of oncoming aircraft.

To these ends, the Air and Air Liaison officers coordinate local artillery and naval fire support in what is known as a SEAD team. After enemy AA positions are located, high intensity suppression fire is concentrated on them as support aircraft run in for the attack. The fire continues as the planes dive on the targets. As the aircraft approach incoming SEAD fire, the salvos are stopped just long enough to enable the air attack to proceed, and then resume at an even higher intensity to afford the aircraft a safe escape.

Such an integrated operation will soon be simplified with the new Marine Integrated Fire and Air Support System (MIFAS), with secured voice and data distribution and much more highly sophisticated as compared to existing systems.

The CH-46 Sea-Knight.

A combined amphibious and heliborne assault.

taining four types of helicopters and, if needed, a selection of fixed-wing aircraft. The helicopters regularly operated by the composite squadron are the Bell AH-1T or AH-1J Cobra gunships, providing direct support for ground forces; UH-1N Hueys, used for command, control and liaison; CH-46 Sea Knights, used for medium troop and supply transport; and several types of CH-53s, used for heavy lift; and

a service group to support the combat forces ashore.

The entire MAU is normally embarked aboard four to seven Navy amphibious ships (depending on mission and ship size) which can support the various components ashore for up to 15 days. The MAU is the most responsive Marine formation; it is positioned in critical tension spots and can react to a deployment order instantaneously; they can fulfill any small-scale, forcible entry mission or support airborne forces already on the ground. Their mere presence can signal American determination, which can add to the deterrence factor. However, the MAU cannot be employed for extended periods without reinforcement as it is mainly a rapid deployment element, a first-line unit with a larger force to follow.

AH-1J helicopter gunship taking off the helicopter carrier.

The new AH-1T, the most advanced helicopter Gunship in the Marine's inventory.

The MAB is structured according to the same principles as the MAU but multiplied approximately three times in strength.

The MAB consists of:

a task-organized regimental landing team, normally of two infantry battalions, each of MAU infantry unit size;

a tank company and an artillery battalion, or, in lighter strength, a Light Assault Vehicle (LAV) company (the first of which was activated with I FMF in 1983);

a combat engineer company, a recce company, an AAV company, and a TOW AT platoon;

an aviation element such as a Marine Aircraft Group (MAG), which may consist of fixed wing aircraft detachments, helicopters squadrons, command and control units, anti-aircraft elements deploying Improved Hawk and Stinger SAMS (now replacing the Redeye), and Vulcan AA guns. This component can operate from both carriers and assault ships, or on shore from expeditionary airfields constructed by special teams; and

a service group capable of supporting the MAB in combat for 30 days.

The MAB can be forward-deployed for extended periods afloat, and when properly utilized, can be deployed for immediate response in no-notice situations. One MAB is currently on station with its equipment in the Southwest Asian area. In amphibious operations, the MAB is also heliportable for the initial assault wave, thus giving an over-the-horizon amphibious capability which would have tremendous impact on a well-defended enemy coast.

The Marine Amphibious Force (MAF)

The largest, heaviest and most powerful Marine assault formation, the MAF, is normally built around an infantry division and an aviation wing, but may range in size from less than one to several divisions. The MAF is capable of large amphibious operations, mainly involving forcible entry with a medium to highly defended coastline. It is also capable of carrying out follow-up operations

ashore subsequent to the initial landing.

Like the MAU and MAB, the MAF is structured according to MAGTF guidelines:

a ground combat element comprised of three infantry brigades (MAB size), an artillery regiment, a tank battalion, an LAV battalion, an AAV battalion (the first of which will become operational in 1984-85), a combat engineer battalion and a recce battalion;

a combat aviation element consisting of a 600+ aircraft wing of fixed and rotary wing aircraft squadrons, anti-aircraft units, command and control units, and other aircraft units, such as those using heavy lift helicopters for rapid force projection; and

combat service support elements including the Force Service Support Group (FSSG) which provides logistics support for the entire force, including supply, maintenance, engineering, motor transport, medical supply etc., and which can sustain the MAF for 60 days.

Several significant improvements will enhance Marine fighting capabilities in the near future. The present Marine AAV is the relatively old, but highly effective LVT (Tracked Landing Vehicle). The LVTP-7 (personnel version) is the only full-track amphibious vehicle in the world capable of operating in rough seas and 10 foot surf. These vehicles are used for assault landings, and, when feasible, in subsequent operations ashore. The USMC currently operates about 985 units of the LVT series. In a Service Life Extension Program (SLEP), the Corps intends to modernize 948 LVTs and add 333 new vehicles of LVT-7A standard.

This vehicle is capable of carrying 25 fully armed Marines plus a three man crew, and is equipped with an all-electric twin-MG turret as compared to the old M85 .50 cal. turret mounted on the LVTP-7. It can stay afloat for seven and a half hours or drive 300 miles on land with diesel fuel stored in two side tanks. The improved model will have a better engine, a VT400 turbo-charged Cummins diesel of almost twice the dis-

The new Light Attack Vehicle, LAV-25, now deployed by the Marines.

Below: LCU landing troops in Lebanon.

Facing page, above: An M-60 tank loaded on an LCU.

placement of the present 300 h.p. engine and rated at 400 h.p. This new powerplant, along with the vehicle's new suspension system, will have the capacity for added weight without degrading performance.

As with present LVTs, two waterjets of 3025lbs thrust each are used both for drive and steering. Organic night vision sights will be included, and two additional universal weapon mounts will be installed on the sides. Two specialized vehicles have also been derived from the basic LVT design. The LVTC command vehicle has such communication sets as the PRC-106, VRC-12 and PRC-75. A remote control switchboard system and intercom is also supplied. New modifications will add PLRS attachments, a new 44 channel switchboard and an M60 machine gun. The LVTC will be modified from 1984 to 1985.

The LVTR recovery machine, one of which is employed with every AAV company, is a utility vehicle equipped for the recovery and maintenance of automotive equipment. LVTR-A1s will have an improved crane with up to 6000lb lift capacity, enough for engine replacement. It will also have a horizontal winching capability of 30,000 ft/lb, enough for pulling an LVTP out of the mud. Two LVTRs are deployed with the battalion's support group, providing first to third echelon basic maintenance.

A new light attack vehicle, the LAV-25, is the Marines' newest weapon system. Based on the Swiss Pirhana and manufactured by General Motors of Canada, this eight-wheeler is equipped with a turretted 25mm Bushmaster Chain Gun which can be used in light assault support. The LAV-25 provides a rapidly deployable weapon system with relatively heavy firepower whose ammunition is capable of perforating the armor of light tanks and all known APCs, including the Soviet BMP. It has a high road speed and good water velocity, as well as good cross country capability. The vehicle's two-man turret is also armed with a coaxial M140 7.62mm MG. A free-mounted M60 7.62 MG also rides on the turret. Advanced night vision equipment includes an infrared fire control system and a night viewer for the driver. Its armor provides protection against small arms and shrapnel; it is also fully NBC protected, with integral detection, decontamination and air purification systems. The Marines have ordered 289 of these vehicles to equip three Light Assault Battalions, and intend to have a total number of 758 LAVs by 1985.

TRAINING

Among the various US armed forces, Marine training is probably the toughest of all. Apart from continuous top-level physical exercise, Marines are drilled in realistic, mission-oriented routines right up to company level. At each Marine base, purposely situated on the coasts, nearby beaches are used for amphibious exercises, with AAVs and, on occasion, amphibious vessels. Combined-arms training is stressed at all levels in which commanders of all ranks exercise the use of available air, naval and artillery fire power.

The most realistic training program is held on the battalion level at the Marine Air-Ground Combat Center (MAGCC) at Twentynine Palms, California. Ten battalions per year, eight of them regular units, undergo exercises in a complete range of Marine missions. A vast desert area enables the full exploitation of speed and power and allows support elements to test their long-range supply efforts. Another training area is the Mountain Warfare Center at Bridgeport, California. Here, Marines learn fighting and survival skills in a mountainous, cold weather environment. Marines also attend the Army's Jungle Warfare School in Panama, which completes the force's range of 'every clime and space' fighting capability.

Command post exercises are held with sophisticated equipment for enhanced realism. An example is the computerized Tactical Warfare Simulator Evaluation and Analysis System (TWSEAS) located at Camp

Above: The LHA-1 Tarawa seen here with helicopters and an open docking well.

Left: A CH-46 seen on the Okinawa (LPH-3).

Below: A US Navy Sea Knight (CH-46) from the USS Sylvania (AFS-2) moves supplies to the Shreveport (LPD-12) flight deck while operating off the Lebanese coast.

Lejeune, Camp Pendleton and the USMC Development Center at Quantico MCAS, Georgia. Using a series of M313 shelters, command personnel at all levels can be trained in simulated combat situations according to unit tasks. All necessary communications, both line and radio, as well as mapping and information distribution, are available as they would be in combat. Information is fed separately to each formation in the exercise as they 'advance'. Time of day, weather, foliage and their effects on visibility, mobility and firepower, are computer simulated. Trainees employ tactics 'by the book' for each situation encountered. Innovative ideas can also be tested here, which is preferable to trying them out in combat. An important training feature of TWSEAS is that it allows the 'nitty gritty' conditions of war, such as surprise enemy moves, logistic breakdowns, etc., to be simulated, something often overlooked in prolonged non-computerized 'wargames'. Commanders must also work day and night, learning to share command duties and shifts, as they would during a real war. The introduction of computers into Marine training does not relieve the commander from operational or tactical decision making; it only makes him think better and become better prepared for the sophistication of the future battlefield.

Marine aviation wings also conduct realistic training exercises at the USMC's Yuma, Arizona-based Weapons and Tactical Training Squadron. Marine aviators also participate in the USAF's Red Flag exercises.

PREPOSITIONED STOCKS
AND WEAPONS

Recognizing the need for improved global mobility while retaining its primary amphibious role, the Marine Corps began to preposition stocks and weapons in several high probability conflict areas. The Mobility Enhancement Initiative, announced in 1979, called for the maritime prepositioning of Marine forces as required for the then-just-established Rapid Deployment Force. Under this program (which followed an earlier scheme undertaken during the early '60s in which prepositioning was considered for five divisions, except that all supplies were consumed by the Vietnam war effort), supplies and weapons for a full MAB were packed on seven ships and stationed at Diego Garcia in the Indian Ocean, the vessels comprising the Near-Term Prepositioned Force (NTPF). The Corps then began forming the 7th MAB for a rapid deployment role in Southwest Asia. The 7th MAB was organized primarily from units of the I FMF and based at Twentynine Palms. Its equipment, pre-positioned with the NTPF, was drawn from I FMF logistical bases in Barstow and included tanks, artillery, AAVs, trucks and jeeps, and enough ammunition, POL, water and supplies to support the MAB for 30 days. The 7th MAB would be airlifted to the contingency area, linking up with its supplies at a friendly port such as Mombasa, Kenya; Berbera, Somalia; Ras Banas, Egypt; or Muscat, Oman. During recent exercises, prepositioned supplies and vehicles were offloaded and tested, with a surprisingly low percentage of malfunctions. Enhancement programs for the prepositioning of a full division's supplies are now underway in the Maritime Prepositioning Ships (MPS) program, which is dealt with in detail in the chapter on sealift. When the program is completed in 1987, prepositioned brigade supplies will be stationed in Southwest and Northeast Asia, and probably in the North Sea or Mediterranean areas as well. For contingencies in other locales, forces can be drawn from CONUS-based units.

It is important to note that neither the NTPF nor the MPS are to replace the amphibious capability of the Marines. The MPS concept requires a 'friendly' environment for unloading. It can take from three to five days to discharge the ships, with a minimum of 12 hours (with only light combat equipment and no logistics support). No such operation could be accomplished by forcible entry, but its supplies could support a follow-on force. Another limitation is the fact that the MPS and the already-deployed NTPF will include only pre-configured and selected stocks, which will not include everything the Marines might have taken had they been launched from their bases. The types of deployment are therefore less flexible than those of a regular Marine task force. But for rapid deployment, the line must be drawn somewhere…

The first MPS brigade was activated in 1984 at Camp Lejeune, with the rest of the brigades to be established in 1985 and 1986. The 7th MAB, with its Diego Garcia prepositioned stocks, will be replaced by another brigade. The land prepositioning of supplies is now being undertaken in Norway, with enough MAB supplies to last 30 days.

Below: A CH-46 delivering an M-102 howitzer from the Saipan.

Left: A Sea Stallion (CH-53) landing on the Guadalcanal.

Left bottom: Sea Knights operating from the Guam (LPH-9) off Grenada.

Amphibious Operations

The crown of US Marine operations is the amphibious landing. It is a most impressive, but complicated task, only rarely undertaken by military planners. It requires top intelligence and utmost care in the coordination and maneuver of combat forces, aviators and seamen.

While the Marines operate the land-end of amphibious operations, the Navy operates the seagoing side of things and gets the Marines across the oceans to the beaches via dedicated amphibious support ships. These vessels are regularly stationed at ports near Marine bases such as San Diego, Norfolk, Pearl Harbor, Subic Bay and Okinawa. Amphibious ships comprise a range of special landing and support vessels of various kinds.

THE BIG GUYS

The LHA-1 (Tarawa-class), five of which have been commissioned, is a 39,300t displacement ship that can make 24 knots. It has a flight deck which can support the simultaneous deployment of nine helicopters and a below-decks 268' x 78' hangar whose clearance allows large helicopters like the CH-46 and CH-53 to be stored. It can carry 12 CH-46s, six CH-53s, four AH-1Js and a number of UH-1 Hueys. With its flight deck and hangar space, the LHA can also deploy with the AV-8A and B-model STOL Harriers, which have

Above: The ammunition ships, part of the support elements.
(USS Nitro, AE-23).

Left: USS Trenton seen leaving Portsmouth while on Mediterranean cruise.

Below left: The USS Raleigh LPD-1) seen in operation with a Harrier STOL aircraft.

Below: The USS Ponce (LPD-15) taking part in NATO exercise in Norway.

Facing page, above, right: The Guadalcanal (LPH-7) loaded with USMC helicopters on station off Beirut.

Right: An LCU leaving the USS Nashville docking well.

been deployed in the Pacific and Indian Oceans and the Mediterranean Sea.

Inside its large docking well, the LHA can accommodate four LCUs for transporting tanks and vehicles ashore, and two LCM-6s for shuttling troops and vehicles. Five elevators handle supply movement from the flight deck level down to the docking well. Overhead monorail cars transfer palletized supplies between the elevators and the landing craft. Forward of the docking well are decks with space for 200 vehicles, including tanks, guns, trucks and AAVs, all the decks being interconnected by ramps. Amphibious vehicles like the LVTP-7 can be launched eight at a time from another well-deck. Each LHA can also carry 2000 troops in addition to its 900 man-crew.

A new version of the LHA, called the LHD-1, is now under construction, with delivery of the first vessel planned for September 1984. These modified LHAs will have increased capability to carry three new LCACs and 1873 troops, with fixed facilities to support up to six AV-8B Harriers and an Intermediate Aviation Maintenance Detachment (IAMD). The LHD will also be able to be converted to a sea control ship, a concept rejected in the late '70s with the Tarawa-class. The LHA (and later the LHD) can also act as an amphibious operation command post, as it is equipped with command and communications facilities and Integrated Tactical Amphibious Warfare Data Systems (ITAWDS) to keep tabs on troop and unit positions. Typical deployment combines an LHA, one or two LSTs, and one LPD to support an MAU.

The LPH (Iwo Jima-class), seven of which are now deployed, was first commissioned in 1961. This is primarily a helicopter support ship equipped with a large deck for VTOL operations. It has an 18,300 ton displacement and is relatively slow, with only a 20 kt cruising speed. The large below-deck hangar accommodates about 20 helicopters of all Marine aviation types, of which five can be launched or recovered simultaneously from the flight deck.

185

Above: The Tarawa seen from within a CH-46.

Left: LST-1188 Saginaw arrives in Beirut.

Below: Two LSTs seen in Beirut bay, the USS Spartanburg county (LST-1193), seen with its "mouth" open. In the background is the USS Fairfax county (LST-1192).

Facing page, above: A rear view of the USS Cleveland (LPD-7), seen with LCMS stationed in the docking well.

Facing page, below: A truck of the 32nd MAU offloaded from the USS Saginaw in Beirut.

The LPD (Raleigh-class), similar to the Tarawa-class, was developed with combined amphibious requirements in mind. A balanced load concept was the basis of its configuration, and the result was a combination of Attack Cargo Ship and Dock Landing Ship (LSD). A 13,900 ton displacement, 20 kt-capable ship, the LPD comprises a docking well occupying only part of the vessel, and a forward section with vehicle decks and troop accommodations. The docking well is relatively small as compared to those of other classes. It can accommodate one LCU and three LCM-6s, or four LCM-8s. Two further LCM-6s and four personnel landing craft can be carried at the aft end of the superstructure and lowered by crane. A landing platform, placed over the well, can support two large helicopters, but the vessel has no shelters for extended chopper deployment. There are accommodations for 840 troops. One of the Raleigh-class ships, the *LaSalle*, was converted into a CENTCOM command ship and is now positioned in the Persian Gulf as part of an MAU.

The LPD-4 (Austin-class), a modification of the Raleigh-class, is a 16,900 ton vessel capable of 20 knots. It comprises enlarged helicopter landing space and hangar accommodations, and a larger docking well with a unique telescopic extension capability of over 80 feet which enables it to trade decks and docking well space according to the mission requirements. Troop accommodation is identical to Raleigh-class ships. The present 11-ship LPD-4 force is planned for a SLEP which will add 15 years to its service life and enable the vessel's continued deployment beyond the year 2000. Among its post-SLEP features will be an area for the deployment of four helicopters, support space for one LCAC, and accommodations for an additional 90 troops.

The LSD-28/LSD36/LSD-41 Thomaston-, Anchorage-, and 41-class Dock Landing Ships. The Thomaston (LSD-28), an 11,270 ton vessel capable of 22.5 knots, is a design used as early as the Korean War. It can accommodate three LCUs or nine

LCM-8s. It is less flexible than modern ships as it has a vehicle deck amidships and a docking-well without direct access from within. Therefore, the LCUs have to be preloaded before entering the well where they are sheltered during the voyage. Loading is handled by two cranes, each capable of lifting 50 tons. A landing pad with space for a single helicopter can be installed aft.

The Anchorage-class (LSD-36) is much improved over the Thomaston. It has docking space for three LCUs or nine LCM-8s, or an alternative load of 50 LVTP-7s. On deck, a single LCM-6 and a personnel and vehicle LC can be carried. But here, too, there is no direct access from the vehicle storage decks to the docking well, and cranes must be used to transfer supplies to the landing craft.

The first of eight new 41-class LSDs, designed to replace the old Thomaston-class ships, was launched in 1984. The LSD-41s have a displacement of 15,745 tons and can make 20 knots. They have a flight deck large and strong enough to accommodate two helicopters as heavy as the CH-53E. Their docking well will be longer, capable of accommodating four new LCACs and also the LCU. The ships have accommodations for 338 troops in addition to the LC unit crews. Construction on a modified version, the LSD-49, with even more area for vehicles and supplies, is planned to begin in 1988. The total number of this class will be 10.

The LST (Newport-class), a Tank Landing Ship of 8,342 ton displacement and 20 knots top speed, is capable of carrying large vehicles such as tanks in a below-deck ramp area of 19000 ft², enough room for 500 tons of combat vehicles. Its distinctive feature is a large, jaw-shaped sling which supports the forward ramp during loading and offloading.

AMPHIBIOUS DEFICIT

With this impressive range of ships, it may seem odd when it is understood that, all together, they can transport only a fraction of the forces the Marines can assign for a given contingency. But in its development plans and ship construction, the Navy is now revitalizing its amphibious capability. The present needs of the Marines to lift an MAF plus an MAB will not be fulfilled until 1994, when new ships will have been added to the fleet. This force will include some 50,000 troops and 633 helicopters, as shown in the following table. According to Marine analysis, the most critical elements will be carried in the Assault Echelon (AE) ships, with more in Assault Follow-on Echelon (AFOE) vessels, and reinforcement troops, vehicles and supplies transported by the Military Sealift Command. The AE will consist of up to 75% of the personnel, over 50% of the vehicles, 20% of the cargo and 10% of POL (petroleum oil and lubricants) storage needed for the assault force. To support this force, the Navy is building a fleet of 74 ships as compared to the present force of 61 amphibious support ships of various classes now available. These forces are now providing a total lift capability shown in the table below.

Right: The USS Spiegel Grove (LSD-32) deploys an experimental version of LCAC, the JEFF-B type. In September, 1984, the first production LCAC rolled off Bell's production line.
Facing page, far right: Landing Craft Assault, LCA. These types were widely used in ww II and were the basic design for today's LCs.
Facing page, center: the new LCAC landing Craft Air Cushion embarking from an LSD-41, an artist's impression of the new capabilities of the USMC.

An artist's concept of the LHD class. The first ship is scheduled to be operational in 1989.

AMPHIBIOUS LIFT CAPABILITY, US NAVY 1984-1994

year	troops	vehicles 1000 ft^2	cargo 1000 ft^3	helicopters (CH-46 equiv.)	landing craft (LCAC)	(LCU)	(LCM-
1984 (total)	40634	791	1720	427	31	14	73
1994 (MAF)	37800	760	1790	467	65	9	38
(MAB)	12200	280	700	166	25	4	16
1994 (total)	50000	1040	2490	633	90	13	54

THE LANDING CRAFT

Assault Landing Craft (LCA)
Used for amphibious assault during World War II, LCAs have been replaced by the modern LVTs in the front line. LCAs turned into LCUs (utility) and LCMs (motorized) are used today for second echelon amphibious transport of artillery and supplies to the beach head. Some are also used to carry tanks, but this is usually done in an area already secured. Basic designs now in USMC service are the LCM-6 and 8, the large LCU, and the successor to the WW II LCA, the LCVP (vehicles and personnel).

Air Cushion Landing Craft (LCAC)
This design has been the dream of military planners for a long time. The LCAC can carry combat equipment such as tanks, LAVs and APCs, or fire-support equipment such as SP guns. The main advantage of the LCAC is its quickness, with a cruise speed of 40kt; an LCAC-supported amphibious attack could be launched from beyond the horizon, with the enemy totaly unaware of the coming force. The LCAC is powered by six gas turbines and can carry over 55 tons of cargo.

US LANDING CRAFT: comparison table

Designation	length	displacement (full)	speed	cargo
LCU-1619	134'	375 tons	8 kt	3 tanks or 170 tons
LCU-1466	119'	360 tons	10 kt	3 tanks or 150 tons
LCU-501	119'	320 tons	10 kt	4 tanks or 200 tons
LCM-8	73'	115 tons	9 kt	1 tank or 60 tons
LCM-6	56'	62 tons	9 kt	80 troops or 34 tons
LCVP	35.8'	13.5 tons	9 kt	4 tons
LCAC	90'	–	40 kt	1 tank or 60 tons

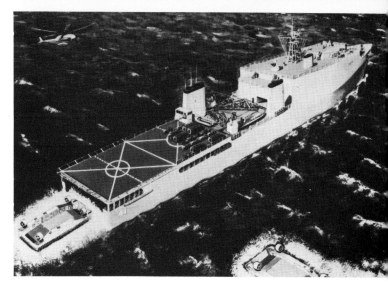

An artist's impression of the LSD-41 class, operating LCACS.

189

Sealift

Above: NTPF ships stationed at Diego Garcia.

Far left: USMC 7 MAB vehicles boarded on the USNS Mercury prior to deployment to the Indian Ocean.

Left: US Marines M-60 tanks boarding the Mercury's Ro/Ro ramp.

Right: EDRE alert! 24th Mechanized Division tanks rush to Savanah port to board MSC ships, which will take them to their assigned deployment area.

Strategic sealift, although less publicized than airlift operations, nevertheless plays a vital part in force projection, especially when locations such as Southwest Asia are concerned. Strategic sealift concerns not only the Marine and Navy forces at sea, but also the various rapid deployment force components from the other services. Recognizing the importance of strategic sealift, the US Navy has recently added this to its previous two objectives, those of sea control and force projection.

In general, sealift is much cheaper and less restricting on cargo size and weight than airlift is, while its most serious deficiency is the longer time it takes and the risks run while travelling unescorted for extended periods during wartime. Typical sealift cargo comprises vehicles, resupply, petroleum oil and lubricants (POL) to support the fighting forces of the Assault Follow-on Echelon (AFOE) and, eventually, reserve troops.

During WW II and the years that followed, all cargo was carried by Navy ships. During the early 1970s, fleet size decreased as ships were phased out. As a result, it was decided that the AFOE would be supported, not by naval ships, but by vessels chartered from merchant fleets. This decision added a further risk to the already dangerous business of forcible entry by amphibious forces.

According to estimates, it must take no more than five days for strategic sealift ships to arrive at their destinations and load supplies for the AFOE. Although Navy decision-makers are presently confident of this capability, they also have doubts for the future. If Marine support were the Sealift Command's only task, things might be easier. But defense concepts call for much larger tasks for its armed forces, with requirements far overreaching existing capabilities. For a Southwest Asian contingency alone, Sealift Command would have to supply almost 95% of the dry cargo and 90% of the POL needs for forces ashore, never mind for naval battle groups, as well as the vessels of nearby fleets.

At present, the Military Sealift Command (MSC) is responsible for all

Above: A ship from the NTPF on station at Diego Garcia. Note its self-sustained offloading capability via the on-board cranes.

Left: The USNS Mercury (TAKR-10) being loaded with supplies and vehicles for the 7 MAB.

Right: TOW jeeps from Echo company, 325th Airborne brigade, 82nd Airborne Division, awaiting to board the USNS Ohio to be shipped to California, part of a simulated SWA deployment during Gallant Eagle 82 exercise.

sealift operations concerning the military. In times of crisis, it would be augmented by privately owned merchant ships. After the sharp decline of the US fleet since WW II (from 2200 to 440 ships in 30 years!) despite growing military needs, the Ready Reserve Fleet (RRF) was established, consisting of ships that could, in times of emergency, add to the Navy's sealift capability already augmented by privately-owned vessels. The RRF's activation could also postpone the call-up of further private ships, therefore limiting damage to the economy. While NATO allies are committed to supporting a European contingency with over 400 ships, and a Northeast Asian crisis with 20, in Southwest Asia the US can rely only on herself for sealift vessels. The RRF force projected for 1988 is 77 ships, 61 of them dry cargo ships and 16 of them tankers. At present, however, the RRF is about 60% short of this number, with only 31 cargo ships and a tanker which can be made available for military utilization within five to 10 days following emergency procedures. While the services can also rely on US-controlled (but not owned) ships during times of war or a limited crisis such as rapid deployment to Southwest Asia, the activation of RRF ships alone would be the best situation that could be expected.

Compared to the fast, modern supertankers and container ships, the US MSC fleet is obsolescent and inefficient. But even the new modern container ships and Roll On/Roll Off (RO/RO) vessels need the special port facilities of friendly nations in order to offload their cargo during military operations, especially in places like the Middle East where the US has no firm base as it does in other areas such as Europe and the Far East.

Improvements and solutions, however, are underway at several shipyards around the US. Converted SL-7 (TAKR) container ships soon to enter service will be able to reach twice the speed of present RRF vessels, about 33 knots. They will be able to arrive in Southwest Asia after a maximum of seven days at sea, as compared to the present three weeks. These vessels will be conventional high speed container ships purchased by the US Navy, and are being modified with more suitable military lift capability. Four of the eight TAKRs will be transformed into highly efficient, partially RO/RO-capable ships. Each vessel will have six RO/RO decks for vehicle storage; the top deck will include a flight deck. The ship will be equipped with cranes for offloading, as well as a ramp system in addition to some limited container capability.

Out of the eight SL-7s now being built, four will be used in rapid deployment roles for forces assigned to CENTCOM's pool. Two will be maintained on ready status near Jacksonville, Florida, to support the 24th Mechanized Division; two more will be stationed at New Orleans to support either the 6th Cavalry or the 101st Air-Assault Division. The rest of the SL-7s will be maintained by the RRF at a high readiness status of five days alert at Philadelphia and San Francisco.

The move from large breakbulk ships to container ships is welcome, but the old designs still allow flexibility. Not every military item can fit into an 8×8 ft. opening; in fact, over 75% of all military cargo is not containerable, and therefore older and slower ships will still be used for sealift purposes for a long time to come. Large platforms, strengthened versions of the commercial racks that fit in the standard container guides on the ship, will be fitted. In essence, flat commercial racks function as portable decks that are loaded and unloaded from container ships with the cargo they carry. As an alternative, the ships can be fitted with large container-size 'sea sheds' that are installed in reinforced container guides and provide a cargo hold much wider and more adaptable for military use. Sea sheds are strong enough to carry the heaviest of military equipment. Once fitted, they can remain on a ship indefinitely. Both strengthened flat racks and sea sheds will be installed on 30 container ships, something which will allow the transfer of a full army division plus its support, without any size or weight restrictions.

One of the NTPF tankers seen on station.

A self sustained cargo ship, loaded with containerized supplies on station with the NTPF.

This civilian Maine class Ro/Ro ship was chartered by the MSC and is now being deployed by the NTPF.

This 33Kt sea-Land (SL) class was converted into the MSC fastest carrier, the SL-7 class TAKR.

The first SL-7, USNS Algol, entered service in September 2 1984, taking part in Reforger exercise.

Another modification will be the installation of replenishment-at-sea equipment on specific ships. This will allow more ships to act in battle group support roles and make other ships available for cargo and POL transport.

The offloading of equipment and supplies will be coordinated with Army and Marine forces which are responsible for the systems and their operation. For offloading at undeveloped ports, specially-equipped crane ships called TACS, which are now being built, will be needed. These ships will enable the conventional container ships to be offloaded without special port facilities. The Navy will also use mobile piers called 'elevated causeways' to help move supplies ashore. These can be installed on a ship within 72 hours. More help will come from transportable barges which will act as ramps from RO/RO ships to the docks.

PREPOSITIONING

In order to shorten the time lapse from boarding to landing, the decision to preposition supplies and weapons was made. It began with the Near Term Prepositioned Force (NTPF), a concept which has grown in numbers since the early '80s, from eight to its present 18 ships stationed near Diego Garcia. This force can deploy from its station relatively quickly, arriving off the Arabian Peninsula in no more than 80 hours. This force stores all the weapons and supplies of the 7th Marine Amphibious Brigade's entire fighting and support strength, as well as the ammunition and supplies for possible army forces deployed in the area. The NTPF force includes three RO/RO ships loaded with various Marine vehicles; five breakbulk ships with supplies, spares and less critical vehicles; four LASH (Lighter-Aboard Ship) vessels with supplies and water purification units; and five POL and water tankers for Navy, Air Force and Army elements. Of all these ships, only five carry the supplies of the 7th MAB. Another ship carries offloading equipment. Other ships carry four 200-bed Marine Corps hospital units.

As a primary mode of rapid deployment, prepositioned unit material is to be offloaded at a service port/beach with an airfield in close proximity. This concept also provides a means to rapidly reinforce previously committed forces, and thus complements amphibious forcible entry capabilities.

For smoother, more reliable operations, a dedicated force called the Maritime Prepositioned Ship program (MPS) was designated. These 13 new vessels (named TAKX) will include the prepositioned weapons and stocks for three Marine Amphibious Brigades. Each force (a squadron of four ships) will be positioned globally at major trouble spots and will be able to sustain the forces ashore for 30 days. The TAKX will be able to discharge all its vehicles and a sixth of its other cargo at a pier in 12 hours, but it may take up to three days to discharge all its cargo. A sample of the storage space is impressive; 150,000 ft^2 for vehicles; 100,800 ft^3 for general storage; 226,000 ft^3 for ammunition; 2,039 ft^2 for drummed POL; 1,523,000 gal of bulk POL; 81,250 gal of potable water; 33 refrigerated rations containers; 2 LCMs; 10 causeways; a side loading tug; four pipe trailers, and 16 hose reels. For only one ship, that is *impressive*. The vessel will be equipped with a helicopter platform, self sustaining unloading equipment (mainly for fluids), and a 40 ton pedestal crane. The total crew while on station will be as many as 70 men, with room for 102 more in temporary accommodations.

All three brigades could also be grouped together to respond to crises in Southwest Asia if needed. The first TAKX is to be completed and positioned by late 1984, with the last of the squadrons due by 1987. This task force will not be stationed at Diego Garcia, but in a region totally removed from the area, probably Northeast Asia.

The US Army has prepositioned weapons and supplies in several parts of the world since the '60s, when it prestocked heavy equipment for four divisions in Europe. Supplies for a fifth and sixth division are to be

At undeveloped ports, the Marines use these floating causeways to deliver their supplies ashore.

198

prepositioned in the Low Countries in the coming years. The stocks are prepared according to Prepositioned Overseas Material Configured in Unit Sets (POMCUS) standards, enabling fast delivery to NATO. Such reinforcement is rated at up to 10 days! Compared to this speed, the infrastructure and availability of reinforcements for Southwest Asia is much less impressive. Prepositioning efforts for this region will have three main objectives: to permit a rapid deployment of forces; to supply materiel needed for the unloading of ships at undeveloped ports; and to provide supplies and ammunition to cover expected initial consumption until CONUS-launched sealift vessels arrive. In this area, the Air Force began in 1984 to preposition aircraft fuel and high-consumed spares aboard NTPF ships.

Management of all the prepositioned supplies will be undertaken by the Joint Deployment System (JDS), which is expected to be working at its full capacity by 1985. The system will provide users more efficient control of available resources prepositioned in the area and the allocation of supplies, scheduled lift requirements and planned force deployment. The new system will hopefully simplify today's complicated inter-arms supplies management in Southwest Asia.

Above: Cutaway of a typical NTPF converted ship. Note the multiple storage decks for vehicles and supplies, containers on-deck and on deck cranes.

Left: To support the task forces, the navy operates tanker/oilers which must keep pace with the fast going fleet.

Right: An artist's concept of what the MPS ship might look like.

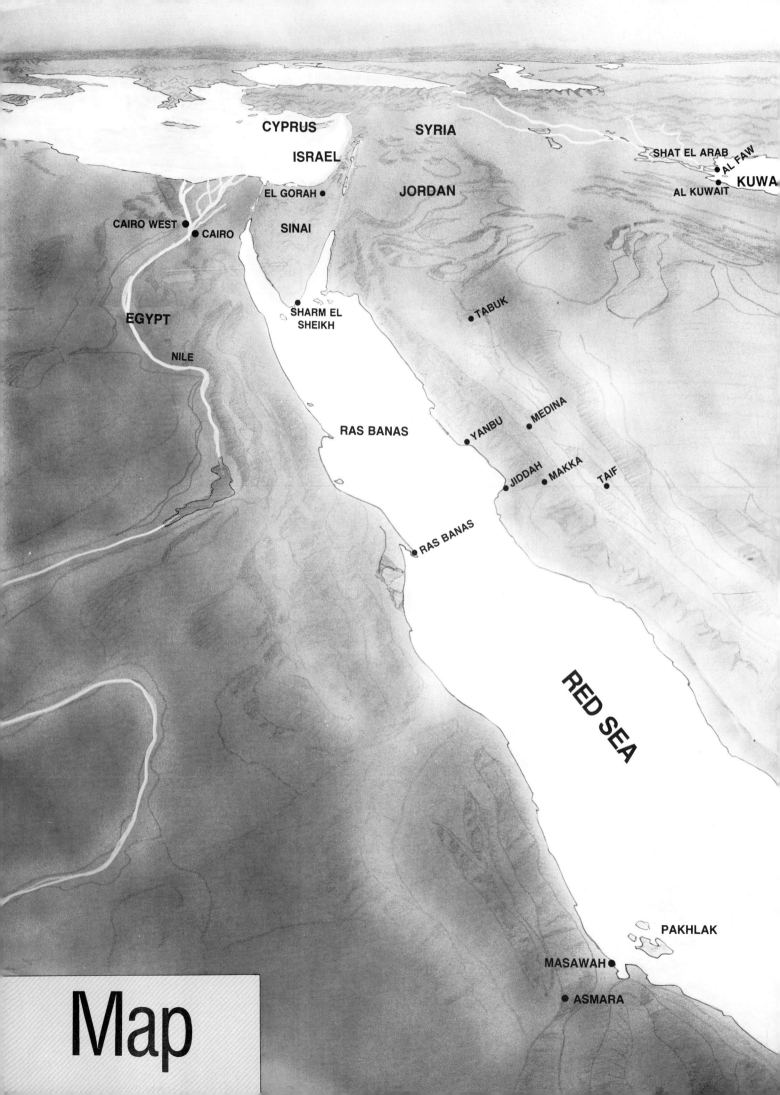

Map

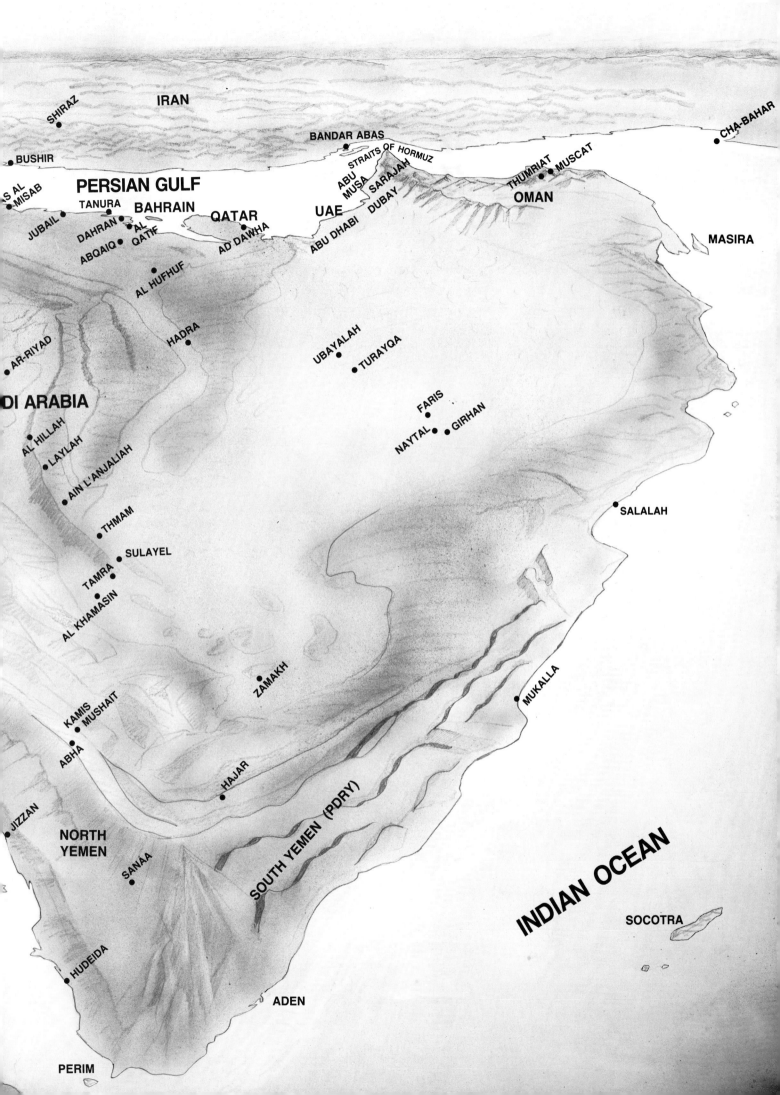

Charts

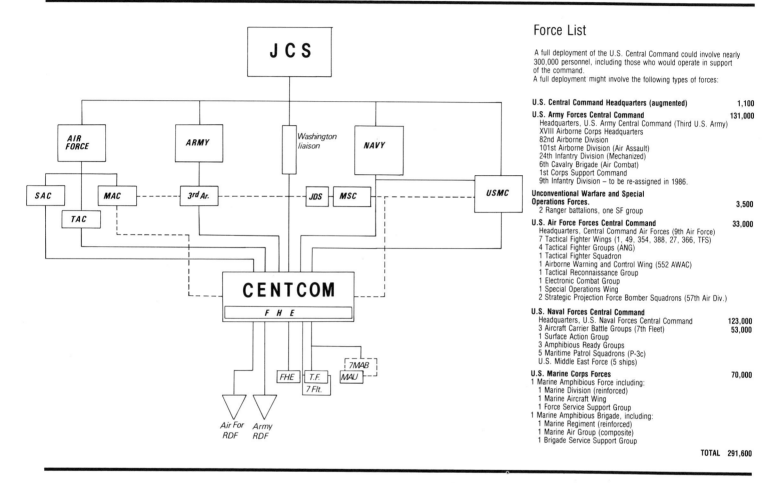

JCS

AIR FORCE

ARMY

Washington liaison

NAVY

SAC

MAC

TAC

3rd Ar.

JDS

MSC

USMC

CENTCOM

F H E

FHE

T.F.
7 Flt.

7MAB

MAU

Air For RDF

Army RDF

Force List

A full deployment of the U.S. Central Command could involve nearly 300,000 personnel, including those who would operate in support of the command.
A full deployment might involve the following types of forces:

U.S. Central Command Headquarters (augmented)	**1,100**
U.S. Army Forces Central Command	**131,000**
Headquarters, U.S. Army Central Command (Third U.S. Army)	
XVIII Airborne Corps Headquarters	
82nd Airborne Division	
101st Airborne Division (Air Assault)	
24th Infantry Division (Mechanized)	
6th Cavalry Brigade (Air Combat)	
1st Corps Support Command	
9th Infantry Division – to be re-assigned in 1986.	
Unconventional Warfare and Special Operations Forces.	**3,500**
2 Ranger battalions, one SF group	
U.S. Air Force Forces Central Command	**33,000**
Headquarters, Central Command Air Forces (9th Air Force)	
7 Tactical Fighter Wings (1, 49, 354, 388, 27, 366, TFS)	
4 Tactical Fighter Groups (ANG)	
1 Tactical Fighter Squadron	
1 Airborne Warning and Control Wing (552 AWAC)	
1 Tactical Reconnaissance Group	
1 Electronic Combat Group	
1 Special Operations Wing	
2 Strategic Projection Force Bomber Squadrons (57th Air Div.)	
U.S. Naval Forces Central Command	
Headquarters, U.S. Naval Forces Central Command	**123,000**
3 Aircraft Carrier Battle Groups (7th Fleet)	**53,000**
1 Surface Action Group	
3 Amphibious Ready Groups	
5 Maritime Patrol Squadrons (P-3c)	
U.S. Middle East Force (5 ships)	
U.S. Marine Corps Forces	**70,000**
1 Marine Amphibious Force including:	
1 Marine Division (reinforced)	
1 Marine Aircraft Wing	
1 Force Service Support Group	
1 Marine Amphibious Brigade, including:	
1 Marine Regiment (reinforced)	
1 Marine Air Group (composite)	
1 Brigade Service Support Group	
TOTAL	**291,600**

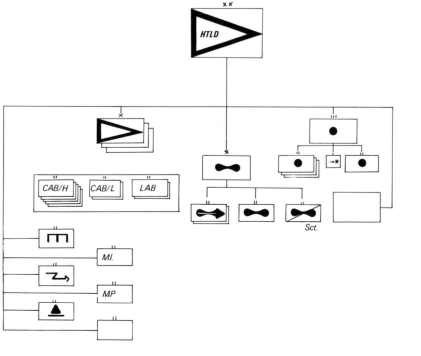

x x

HTLD

x

x

CAB/H

CAB/L

LAB

Sct.

MI.

MP

THE MAGTF
(TYPICAL TASK ORGANISATION*)

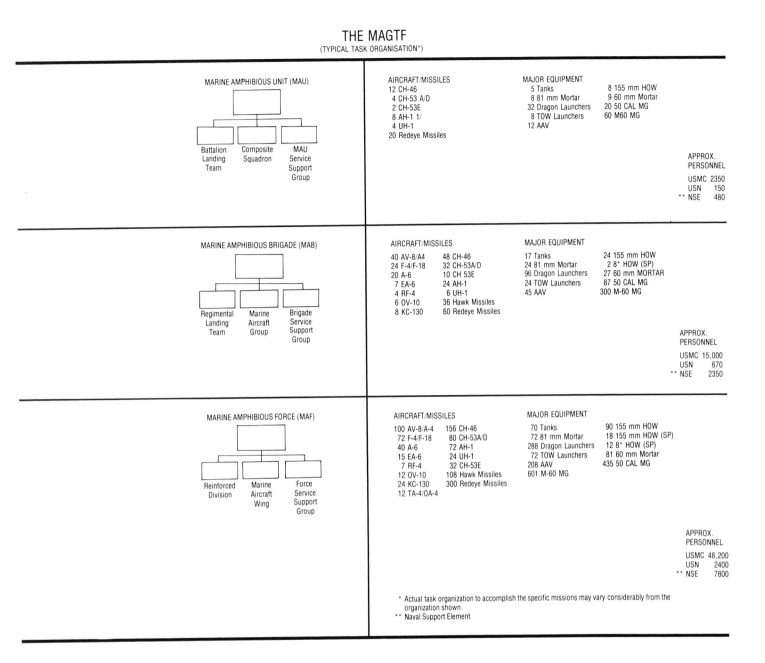

MARINE AMPHIBIOUS UNIT (MAU)

Battalion Landing Team | Composite Squadron | MAU Service Support Group

AIRCRAFT/MISSILES
12 CH-46
4 CH-53 A/D
2 CH-53E
8 AH-1 1/
4 UH-1
20 Redeye Missiles

MAJOR EQUIPMENT
5 Tanks
8 81 mm Mortar
32 Dragon Launchers
8 TOW Launchers
12 AAV

8 155 mm HOW
9 60 mm Mortar
20 50 CAL MG
60 M60 MG

APPROX. PERSONNEL

USMC 2350
USN 150
** NSE 480

MARINE AMPHIBIOUS BRIGADE (MAB)

Regimental Landing Team | Marine Aircraft Group | Brigade Service Support Group

AIRCRAFT/MISSILES
40 AV-8/A4   48 CH-46
24 F-4/F-18   32 CH-53A/D
20 A-6   10 CH 53E
7 EA-6   24 AH-1
4 RF-4   6 UH-1
6 OV-10   36 Hawk Missiles
8 KC-130   60 Redeye Missiles

MAJOR EQUIPMENT
17 Tanks
24 81 mm Mortar
96 Dragon Launchers
24 TOW Launchers
45 AAV

24 155 mm HOW
2 8" HOW (SP)
27 60 mm MORTAR
87 50 CAL MG
300 M-60 MG

APPROX. PERSONNEL

USMC 15,000
USN 670
** NSE 2350

MARINE AMPHIBIOUS FORCE (MAF)

Reinforced Division | Marine Aircraft Wing | Force Service Support Group

AIRCRAFT/MISSILES
100 AV-8/A-4   156 CH-46
72 F-4/F-18   80 CH-53A/D
40 A-6   72 AH-1
15 EA-6   24 UH-1
7 RF-4   32 CH-53E
12 OV-10   108 Hawk Missiles
24 KC-130   300 Redeye Missiles
12 TA-4/OA-4

MAJOR EQUIPMENT
70 Tanks
72 81 mm Mortar
288 Dragon Launchers
72 TOW Launchers
208 AAV
601 M-60 MG

90 155 mm HOW
18 155 mm HOW (SP)
12 8" HOW (SP)
81 60 mm Mortar
435 50 CAL MG

APPROX. PERSONNEL

USMC 48,200
USN 2400
** NSE 7800

* Actual task organization to accomplish the specific missions may vary considerably from the organization shown.
** Naval Support Element

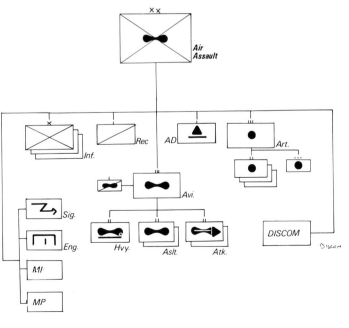

Index

Glossary

Bibliography

HTLD = High Technology Light Division
HTTB = High Technology Test Bed

IAMD = Intermediate Aviation Maintenance Detachment
IFV = Infantry Fighting Vehicle
IRC = Initial Ready Company
ITAWDS = Integrated Tactical Amphibious Warfare Data System
ITV = Improved Tow Vehicle (M-901)

JAAT = Joint Air-Attack Team
JCS = Joint Chiefs of Staff
JDS = Joint Deployment Agency
JVX = Joint services, advanced Vertical lift aircraft
LAB = Light Attack Battalion
LACT = Light Air Cavalry Troop
LAMPS = Light Airborne Multipurpose System
LAPES = Low Altitude Parachute Extraction System
LAV = Light Armored Vehicle
LCA = Landing Craft Assault
LCAC = Landing Craft Air Cushion
LCM = Landing Craft Motor-vehicles
LCU = Landing Craft Utility
LMI = Light Motorized Infantry
LVT = Landing Vehicle, Tracked
LVTP = —"—, Personnel
LVTR = —"—, Recovery
LVTC = —"—, Command
MAB = Marine Amphibious, Brigade
MAC = Military Airlift Command
MAF = Marine Amphibious Force
MAG = Marine Aircraft Group
MATS = Military Air Transport Command
MAU = Marine Amphibious Unit
MAW = Marine Air Wing
MCM = Counter-Measures
MCAS = Marine Corps Air Station
MEDEVAC = Medical Evacuation
MFO = Multinational Force and Observers
MG = Machine Gun
MLRS = Multiple Launch Rocket System
MPS = Maritime Preposition Ship
MSC = Military Sealift Command
MTT = Mobile Training Team
NAVSTAR = Navigation Satellite Timing And Ranging
NTPF = Near Term Prepositioned Force
NOE = Nap Of the Earth (flight)

OSS = Office of Strategic Services

PIVADS = Product Improvement Vulcan Air Defence System
PLADS = Parachute Low Altitude Delivery System
PLO = Palestine Liberation Organization
PLRS = Position Location Reporting System
POL = Petroleum, Oil, Lubricants

POMCUS = Pre Positioned Overseas Material Configured in Unit Sets
PT = Physical Training

RAT = Rapid Arm and Refuel Team
RDF = Rapid Deployment Force
RDJTF = Rapid Deployment Joint Task Force

RRF = Ready Reserve Fleet
SAC = Strategic Air Force
SAM = Surface/Air Missile
SEAD = Suppression of Enemy Air Defense
SF = Special Forces
SFG = Special Forces Group
SINCGRASS = Single-Channel Ground and Airborne System
SLEP = Service Life Extension Porgram
SOW = Special Operations Wing
SPF = Strategic Projection Force
STOL = Short Take Off and Landing

TAC = Tactical Air Command
TFS = Tactical Fighter Squadron
TFTS = —"— —"— Training Squadron
TFW = Tactical Fighter Wing
TRAM = Target Recognition Multisensor System

UAE = United Arab Emirates
UHF = Ultra High Frequency
USNS = U.S. Naval Ship
USS = U.S. Ship
UV = Unconventional Warfare

VHF = Very High Frequency
VTOL = Vertical Take Off and Landing

For further reading on specific subjects we recommend the following sources: (entries marked with ★ are congressional hearings/statements.)

SCENARIO:
'Navy widens alert area to protect ships', Air-force Times 6 Feb. 1984, by Tom Burgess.
'Terrorism: what to do?', Washington Times, 20 Feb. 1984 Stuart Malawer
'International Terrorism' special edition, The Police Chief, March 1984.
★'Fy 85 security assistance in East Asia' statement of Mr. James A. Kelly, March 22, 1984
'The Mid East Military Balance', M. Heler, Tel Aviv University.

CENTCOM:
'The US Central Command', Defense 84, By Lt. General Robert C. Kingston
★'Status of CENTCOM' Statement of Lt. General Robert C. Kingston, February 23, 1984
'Annual report to the congress' Fy82, 83, 84, 85 Caspar W. Weinberger, Sec. of Defense
'Military posture' Fy 82, 83, 84, 85 by the organization of the Joint Chiefs of Staff
'Gallant Eagle 82 – RDF in action' Defence Update international, Number 28, 'Gallant Eagle' Fact sheet, by the US RDJTF, 1982.
'ADA take part in Gallant Eagle' Air Defense Bulletin, April 82
'The Rapid Deployment Force – fact or fiction?' RUSI journal, June 1981, by Dr. E. Asa Bates.
'RDJTF special update' Defence Update International number 31
★'US readiness command' statement of General Wallace H. Nutting, 23 February 1984/ Maj. General William E. Klein, statement before the armed services subcommittee on manpower and personnel, 6 March 1984
'Soviet Military Power 1981, 83, 84' published by the DOD.
'The Middle East Military survey' 1981 War Data number 8, 9, by David Eshel, Eshel Dramit.
'The Middle East 1982' special edition, Defence Update international 1982,
'Middle East military balance, 1984' Special edition, Defence Update international.
'Global flexibility' Marine Corps Gazette, September 1982, by Brig. General M.K. Sheridan
'The Lebanon experience' Marine Corps Gazette, February 1983, by Colonel James M. Mead
'Diego Garcia' RUSI journal, June 1981, by Sqn Leader J. Clementson, MA
'Jumping into a hot DZ, Grenada 83' Defence Update International number 46, 1983 by Tamir Eshel

GROUND FORCES:
'Toward a new amphibious tactical concept' Marine Corps Gazette July 83, By Colonel R.B. Roythwell
'Amphibious assault craft' National Defence, by Carl White
'Elite fighting units' arco publishing, 1984, by Lt. Colonel David Eshel.

'Fast attack vehicle' Defence Update International, number 51, By Tamir Eshel
'High Technology Light Division' Defence Update International Number 47 & 51, By Tamir Eshel

AIR POWER:
★'Air force readiness' Presentation by Brig. General Mark J. Worrick. March 1984
★'Readiness of the USAF' statement by Lt. General John T. Chain. 1 March 1984
'AV-8B Harrier II' Defence Update 53
★'Military Airlift Command', presentation by General Thomas M. Ryan Jr. 27 March 1984
'Strategic Mobility' Special AUSA report, 1984
'The compelling requirement for combat airlift' Air University Review Aug. 82, Colonel Alan L. Gropman

NAVAL POWER:
★'Naval threat' Statement by Rear admiral John L. Butts, USN, 28 February 1984
★'Amphibious forces' Vice admiral Robert L. Walters, USN. 28 March 1984
★'US Navy readiness' Statement by Vice Admiral James A. Lyons Jr.
★'The Pacific area' statement by Admiral Robert L. Long, USN, 8 March, 1984
★'The US Navy Ready Reserve Force program' Statement of Rear Admiral Richard C. Avrit, USN, 3 april 1984
★'Strategic Sealift' Statement of Rear Admiral Richard C. Avrit, US Navy
'The Naval reserve – vital to Navy missions' National Defense february 1984, by Floyd D. Kennedy Jr.
★'The importance of the US merchant marine to this nation's strategic mobility', Statement by Vice Admiral William H. Rowen, USN, 8 February 1984
★'Sealift programs' Statement of Vice Admiral William J. Cowhill, US Navy.

Acknowledgements

This book is the culmination of a research period of three years, during which myself and my son, Tamir, spent many days visiting the various units, at home, during exercises and in their command centers. We followed the RDF becoming a unified command with the help of many information offices, carefully analizing each step in the evolution of the command. Fortunately, many commanders were interested in our outsider view not less then we were interested in what they had to say, and we hope this book will give this added dimension to them as well as to the readers. We would like to take this opportunity to thank all those who helped us. Especially we would like to thank Commander Joleen K. Keefer, US Navy, and the US Embassy in Tel Aviv, without their cooperation and help, this whole project could not become a reality. Many thanks to the public affairs units of the 82nd Airborne division, 101st Air Assault, XVIII Airborne Corps, 9 Infantry Division, the 2/75 Ranger Battalion, JFK Special Warfare school, Military Airlift Command, Second Marine Division, Central Command, Strategic Air-Force and 7 MAB for their hospitality, and assistance in our visits.

I would also like to personally thank those who were willing to contribute some of their time and ideas to this project:

Lt. General Robert C. Kingston, CENTCOM
Lt. General P.X. Kelly, USMC
Maj. General Jack B. Farris Jr., US Army XVIII Corps
Maj. General James E. Thompson, 101st Air Assault Div.
Maj. General Edward L. Trobaugh, US Army 82nd ABD
Maj. General Alfred M. Gray Jr. 2nd Div. USMC
Brig. General Ellis D. Parker, 101st Air Assault Div.
Brig. General Tzraskoma, USAF MAC
Brig. Gen. Joseph E. Hopkins, 2nd Div. USMC
Brig. General Joseph B. Knotts, 7 MAB, USMC
Brig. General Winglass, 2nd Div. USMC
Brig. General Leo W. Smith II, USAS SAC
Brig. General James W. Crysel 101st Air Assault Div.
Captain Richard D. Milligan, USS New Jersey (USN)
Colonel Bobby H. Freeman 101st Aviation Battalion
Colonel Herbert M. Wassom 101st Air Assault Div.
Colonel Laurence R. Gadoury, US Army
Colonel Cate, 2nd Div. USMC
Colonel Hewitt and Colonel Curter, 101st Air Assault
Colonel Cincotti, JFK center
Lt. Colonel Jack Easton, US Army
Lt. Col T. D. Stouffer, 2nd Div. USMC
Lt. Col. David H. Burpee and Col. Baker, CENTCOM
Lt. Col. Straddler, 2nd Div. USMC
Lt. Col. Louis Bouault, ADEA
Lt. Col Pat Cannon, XVIII corps

Major Roy, 101st Air Assault
Major Robert M. Henslar, US Army 2/75 Ranger
Major Jim Curter, SOCOM
Major Dale Bird, USMC
Captain Al Havrilla, 91D, US Army
Captain Neel, 6th Air Cavalry PR,
Captain Redfern and Captain Butler, 101st Div.
Captain Olson, Air Assault School
Captain Ritch & Captain Duffy, (SOCOM)
Captain Grisson and Captain O'Connor, 91D
S/Mjr James E. Voyies, and S/Sjt Sullivan and F/Sjt Conrad, US 2/75th Rangers M/Sjt M. Pidding, MAC, USAF
CWO Ron Fraizer, 7MAB, USMC
Tom Streeter, US Navy correspondent,

Dr. Vi Ron, Tel Aviv University
Mr. Joseph Kostiner, Shiloah institute.
Mr. Casey Cox, ADEA's 'Skunk works'
Mr. Vogt, Air-Assault museum.

I would also like to thank the various DOD offices which supplied us with many photographs needed for the job, especially to:
Mrs. Bettie E. Sprigg and Mr. Ad Miholsky, Mr. Bob Carlisle, and Lt. Colonel Joseph P. Hollis Jr. from the Pentagon's audiovisual branches.
Mr. David R. Wilson, Mrs. Anna Urband, and Lt. Colonel Eric M. Solander from the magazine/book branches as well as Mr. L. R. Ranger and Mrs. Fuller from MSC and MAC public affairs.

Lt. Col David Eshel (Ret)
Editor

Photo credits:
Most of the photos in this book are credited to the following US armed forces branches:
US Army/ US Air Force/ US DOD/ US Navy/ US MSC/ 82nd Airborne Div./ 101st Air Assault Div./ 9th Infantry Div./ US Marines/ US Special Operations Command/ Strategic Air Command.
Selected photos are taken from various agencies such as:
Camera Press: 21
MG Photographers: 180
Soldier Magazine: 10
AP: 11

Other photos are taken from the private collection of Tamir Eshel and Defence Update Magazine.